Lessons in Truth

LESSONS IN TRUTH

A Course of Twelve Lessons in Practical Christianity

BY

H. EMILIE CADY

AUTHOR OF
"FINDING THE CHRIST IN OURSELVES;" "ONENESS WITH GOD,"
AND "'NEITHER DO I CONDEMN THEE;" "GOD'S HAND,"
AND "LOOSE HIM AND LET HIM GO;" AND
"TRUSTING AND RESTING."

UNITY SCHOOL OF CHRISTIANITY
KANSAS CITY, MISSOURI
1919

43 * 120

CONTENTS

STATEMENT OF BEING

WHO AND WHAT GOD IS—WHO AND WHAT MAN IS

FIRST LESSON

[In entering upon this course of instruction let each one, as far as possible, lay aside for the time being all previous theories and beliefs. By so doing you will be saved the trouble of trying all the way through the course to force "new wine into old bottles." If there is anything as we proceed which you do not understand or agree with, just let it lie passively in your mind until you receive the entire course, for many statements which would naturally arouse antagonism and discussion will be clear and easily accepted a little further on. After the course is completed, if you wish to return to your old beliefs and ways of living, you are at perfect liberty to do so. But for the time being, be willing to become as little children; for, said a Master in spiritual things, "Except ye become as little children ye can in no wise enter the kingdom of heaven." If at times there seems to be repetition, please remember that these are lessons, not lectures.]

When Jesus was talking with the Samaritan woman at the well, he said to her, "God is Spirit; and they that worship him must worship him in spirit and in truth." He did not say, God is *a* Spirit. The article *a*, italicized as it is in our Bibles, has been interpolated by translators. To say "a spirit"

5

would be implying the existence of more than one spirit. Jesus in his statement did not do this.

Webster in his definition of Spirit says, "Spirit is life or intelligence conceived of entirely apart from physical embodiment. It is vital essence, force, energy, as distinct from matter."

God, then, is not, as many of us have been taught to believe, a big personage or man residing somewhere in a beautiful region in the sky called "heaven," where good people go when they die and see him clothed with ineffable glory; nor is he a stern, angry judge only waiting an opportunity somewhere to punish bad people who have failed to live a perfect life here.

God is Spirit, or the Creative energy which is the cause of all visible things. God as Spirit is the invisible life and intelligence (according to Webster's definition of Spirit) which underlies all physical things. There could be no body, or visible part, to anything unless there was first Spirit as creative cause.

God is not a being or person having life, intelligence, love, power. God is that invisible, intangible, but very real something we call Life. God is perfect Love and infinite Power. God is the sum total of these combined, the sum total of all good, whether manifested or unexpressed.

There is but one God in the universe, but one source of all the different forms of life or intelligence we see, whether they be man, animal, tree or rock.

God is Spirit. We cannot see Spirit with these fleshly eyes; but when we clothe ourselves with the spiritual body, then Spirit is visible or manifest and we recognize it. You do not see the living, thinking "me" when you look at my body. You see only the form through which I am manifesting.

God is Love. We cannot see love, nor grasp any comprehension of what love is, except as love is clothed with a body. All the love there is in the universe is God. The love between husband and wife, between parents and children, is just the least little bit of God as pushed forth through visible form into manifestation. A mother's love, so infinitely tender, so unfailing, is the same love, only manifested in greater degree through the mother.

God is Wisdom or Intelligence. All the wisdom or intelligence we see in the universe is God—is wisdom projected through a visible form. To educate (from *educere*, to lead forth) never means to force into from the outside, but always means *to draw out from within something already existing there*. God as infinite wisdom or intelligence lives within every human being, only waiting to be led forth or drawn out into manifestation. This is true education.

. Heretofore we have sought knowledge and help from outside sources, not knowing that the source of all knowledge, the very Spirit of Truth, was lying latent within ourselves, each and every one, only waiting to be called on to teach us the truth about all things—most marvelous of teachers, and everywhere present, without money or price!

God is Power. Not simply God has power, but God *is* Power. In other words, all the power there is to do anything is God. God, the source of our existence every moment, is not simply omnipotent (all powerful); he is Omnipotence (all power). He is not alone omniscient (all knowing); he is Omniscience (all knowledge). He is not only omnipresent, but more—Omnipresence. God is not a being having qualities, but he is the Good itself. Everything you can think of that is good, when in its absolute perfection, goes to make up that invisible being we call God.

God, then, is the Substance (from *sub*, under, and *stare*, to stand), or the real thing standing under every visible form of life, love, intelligence or power. Each rock, tree, animal, everything visible, is a manifestation of the One Spirit—God—differing only in degree of manifestation; and each of the numberless modes of manifestation, or individualities, however insignificant, contains the whole.

One drop of water taken from the ocean is just as perfect ocean water as the whole great body. The constituent elements of water are exactly the same, and they are combined in precisely the same ratio or perfect relation to each other, whether we consider one drop, a pailful, a barrelful or the entire ocean out of which the lesser quantities are taken; each is complete in itself; they differ only in quantity or degree. Each contains the whole; and yet no one would make the mistake of supposing from this statement that each drop was the entire ocean.

So we say that each individual manifestation of God contains the whole; not for a moment meaning that each individual is God in his *entirety*, so to speak, but that each is God come forth, shall I say? in different quantity or degree.

Man is the last and highest manifestation of this Divine Energy, the fullest and most complete expression (or pressing out) of God. To him, therefore, is given the dominion over all other manifestations.

God is not only the Creative Cause of every visible form of intelligence and life at its commencement, but each moment throughout its existence he lives within every created thing as the life, the ever-renewing, recreating, upbuilding cause of it. He never is and never can be for a moment separated from his creations. Then how can even a sparrow fall to the ground without his knowledge? "And ye are of more value than many sparrows."

God *is*. Man exists (from *ex*, out of, and *sistare*, to stand forth). Man stands forth out of God.

Man is a threefold being, made up of spirit, soul and body. Spirit, our innermost, real being, the absolute part of us, the "I" of us, which you and I know has never changed, though our thoughts and circumstances may have changed hundreds of times —this part of us is a standing forth of God into visibility. It is the Father in us. At this central part of his being every person can say, "I and the Father are one," and speak only absolute truth.

Mortal mind—that which Paul calls "carnal mind"—is the consciousness of error.

The great whole of as yet unmanifested Good, or God, from whom we are projections or "off-spring," and "in whom we live, move, and have our being" continually, is to me the Father—*Our Father;* "and all ye are brethren," because all are manifestations of one and the same Spirit. Jesus,

recognizing this, said, "Call no man upon the earth
your father, for one is your Father which is in heav-
en." As soon as any of us recognize our true relationship to all men we at once slip out of our narrow,
personal loves, our "me and mine," into the universal
love which takes in all the world, joyfully exclaim-
ing, "Who is my mother? who are my brethren?
Behold, these are my mother and my brethren!"

Childlike, untrained minds say God is a personal
being. The statement that God is Principle chills
them, and in terror they cry out, "They have taken
away my Lord, and I know not where they have
laid him!"

Broader and more learned minds are always
cramped by the thought of God as a person, for
personality limits to place and time.

God is both Principle and Person. As the creative underlying cause of all things, he is Principle,
impersonal; as expressed in each individual, he becomes personal to that one—a personal, loving, all-
giving Father-Mother. All that any human soul can
ever need or desire is the infinite Father-principle,
the great reservoir of unexpressed good. There is
no limit to the Source of our being, nor to his willingness to manifest more of himself through us, when
we are willing to do his will.

Hitherto we have turned our hearts and efforts toward the external for fulfillment of our desires and for satisfaction, and all have been grievously disappointed. For the hunger of every one for satisfaction is only the cry of the homesick child for its Father-Mother—God. It is only the Spirit's desire in us to come forth into our consciousness as more and more perfection until we shall have become *fully* conscious of our oneness with All-Perfection. Man never has been and never can be satisfied with anything less.

We each have direct access through the Father in us—the central "I" of our being—to the great whole of life, love, wisdom, power, which is God. What we now want to know is, how to receive more from the Fountainhead and to make more and more of God (which is but another name for All-Good) manifest in our daily lives.

There is but one Source of Being. That Source is the living Fountain of All-Good, be it life, love, wisdom, power, or whatever—the Giver of all good gifts. That Source and you are connected every moment of your existence. You have power to draw upon this Source for all of good you are, or ever will be, capable of desiring.

THINKING

We learned in the first lesson that the real substance within everything we see is God; that all things are one and the same Spirit in different degrees of manifestation; that all the various forms of life are just the same as one Life come forth out of the invisible into visible forms; that all the intelligence and wisdom there is in the world is God as Wisdom in various degrees of manifestation; that all the love which people feel and express to others is just a little, so to speak, of God as Love come into visibility through the human form.

Now, when we say there is but one Mind in the entire universe, and that this is the Mind which is God, some persons, having followed understandingly the first lesson, and recognized God as the one Life, one Spirit, one Power, pushing itself out into various degrees of manifestation through people and things, will at once say, "Yes, that is all plain."

But some one else will say, "If all the Mind there is, is God, then how can I think wrong thoughts, or any but God thoughts?"

The connection between the Universal Mind and our own individual minds is one of the most difficult things to put into words, but when it once dawns upon one it is so easily seen.

There is in reality only one Mind (or Spirit, which is life, intelligence, etc.) in the universe; and yet there is a sense in which we are individual, or separate—a sense in which we are free wills and not puppets.

Man is made up of spirit, soul and body. Spirit is the central unchanging *I* of us, the part which since infancy has never changed, and to all eternity never will change. That which Christian Scientists call "mortal mind," is the region of the intellect, where we do conscious thinking and are free wills. This part of our being is in constant process of changing.

In our descent, or outspringing, from God into the material world, spirit is inner—next to God; soul is the clothing, as it were, of the spirit; body is yet the external clothing of soul. And yet all are in reality one, which makes up the man—as steam at the center, water next, and ice as an external, all one, only in different degrees of condensation. In thinking of ourselves we must not separate spirit, soul and body, but rather hold all as one, if we would be strong and powerful. Man originally lived consciously in the spiritual part of himself. He fell by descending in his consciousness to the external or more material part of himself.

"Mortal mind," the term so much used and so distracting to many, is the error consciousness, which gathers its information through the five senses from the outside world. It is what Paul calls "carnal mind" in contradistinction to spiritual mind; and he flatly says: "To be carnally minded [or to believe what the carnal mind says] is death [sorrow, trouble, sickness]; but to be spiritually minded [*i. e.*, to be able to still the carnal mind and let the Spirit speak within us] is life and peace."

The Spirit within you is the Divine Mind, the *real* mind, for without it the mortal mind disappears, just as a shadow, which looks so very real, disappears when the real thing which casts it is removed.

If you find this subject of mortal mind and Universal Mind puzzling to you, do not worry over it, and above all things do not discuss it; but just drop if for a time, and as you go on with the lessons you will find that some day it will all flash suddenly upon you with perfect clearness.

There are today two classes of people, so far as mentality goes, who are seeking deliverance out of their sickness, trouble and unhappiness, through spiritual means. One class requires that every statement made be proved by the most elaborate and logical argument, before they can or will receive it. The other class is willing at once to "become as a little child" and just be taught how to take the first steps toward pure understanding (or knowledge of Truth as God sees it), and then receive the light by direct revelation from the Good. Both are seeking and eventually will reach the same goal, and neither is to be condemned.

If you are one who seeks and expects to get any realizing knowledge of spiritual things through argument or reasoning, no matter how scholarly your attainments or how great you are in worldly wisdom, you are a failure in spiritual understanding. You are attempting an utter impossibility—that of crowding the Infinite into the quart measure of your own intellectual capacity.

"The natural man receiveth not the things of the Spirit of God: for they are foolishness unto him: neither can he know them, because *they are spiritually discerned*." Eventually you will find that you are only beating all around on the outside of the "kingdom of heaven," though in close proximity to it, and you will then become willing to let your intellect take the place of the "little child," without which no man can enter in.

"Eye hath not seen, nor ear heard, neither have entered into the heart of man, the things which God hath [not *will*] prepared for them that love him.

"But God hath revealed them unto us by his Spirit."

"For what man knoweth the things of a man, save the spirit of man which is in him? even so the things of God knoweth no man, but the Spirit of God."

For all those who must wade through months and perhaps years of this purely intellectual or mental process there are today many books to help, and many purely metaphysical teachers who are doing noble and praiseworthy work in piloting these earnest seekers after truth and satisfaction. To them we cry, All speed!

But we, believing with Paul that "the foolishness of God is wiser than men," and that each soul has direct access to all there is in God, are writing for the "little children" who are willing at once, without question or discussion, to accept and try a few plain, simple rules, such as Jesus taught the common people, who heard him gladly—rules by which they can find the Christ (or Divine) within them-

selves, and through it each man for himself work out
his own salvation from all his troubles.

In other words, there is a short cut to the top of
the hill; and while there is a good but long, round-
about road for those who need it, we prefer the less
laborious means of attaining the same end—by seeking directly the Spirit of Truth promised to dwell *in
us* and to lead us into all truth. Our advice is, if
you want to make rapid progress in growth toward
spiritual understanding, stop reading many books.
They only give you some one's opinion about truth,
or are a sort of history of the author's experience in
seeking truth. What you want is *revelation of truth
in your own soul*, and that will never come through
the reading of many books.

Do not even discuss these lessons with others.
Go alone. Think alone. Seek light alone, and if
it does not come at once, do not be discouraged and
run off to someone else to get light; for, as we said
before, by so doing you get only the opinion of the
intellect (false mind), and may be then farther
away from the truth you are seeking than ever before; for the carnal, or mortal mind makes false reports.

The very Spirit of Truth is at your call—within
you. "The anointing ye have received abideth *in*

you." Seek it. Wait patiently for it to "guide you into all truth about all things."

"Let this mind be in you, which was also in Christ Jesus." This is the Universal Mind which makes no mistakes. Still the intellect for the time being, and let it speak to you; and when it speaks, though it be but a "still, small voice," you will know what it says is truth.

How will you know? You will know just as you know you are alive. All the argument in the world to convince you against truth which comes to you through direct revelation will fall flat and harmless at your side. And the truth which you know, not simply believe, you can use to help others. That which comes forth through your spirit will reach the very innermost spirit of him to whom you speak.

What is born from the outside or intellectual perception reaches only the intellect of him you would help.

The intellect, or false mind, which is servant to the Real Mind, and as servant (but not as master) is good, loves to argue; but as its information is based on the evidence of the senses and not on the true thoughts of the Divine Mind in us, it is very fallible and full of error.

Intellect argues. Spirit takes of the deep things

of God, and *reveals*. One may be true; the other always is true. Spirit does not give opinions about truth; it *is* truth, and reveals itself.

Someone has truly said that the merest child who has learned from the depth of his soul to say "Our Father" is infinitely greater than the most intellectual man who has not yet learned it. Paul was a man of gigantic intellect, learned in all the law, a Pharisee of the Pharisees; but after he was spiritually illumined he wrote, "The foolishness of God is wiser than men, and the weakness of God is stronger than men."

Now, it does make a great difference in our daily lives what we as "mortal minds" think about God, about ourselves, about our neighbors. Heretofore, through ignorance of our real selves and of the results of our thinking, we have let our thoughts flow out at random. Our minds have been turned toward the external of our being, and nearly all our information has been gotten through its five senses. We have thought wrong because misinformed by these senses, and our troubles and sorrows are the results of our wrong thinking.

"But," says some one, "I do not see how my thinking evil or wrong thoughts about God, or about any one, can make me sick or my husband lose his position."

Well, I will not just now try to explain all the mental machinery by which bad results follow false thinking, but I will just ask you to try thinking true, right thoughts awhile, and see what the result will be.

Take the thought, "God loves me, and approves of what I do." Think these words over and over continually for a few days, trying to realize that they are true, and see what the effect will be on your body and circumstances.

First, you get a new exhilaration of mind, with a great desire and a sense of power to please God; then a quicker, better circulation of blood, with sense of pleasant warmth in the body, followed by better digestion, etc. Later, as the truth flows out through your being into your surroundings, everybody will begin to manifest a new love for you without your knowing why; and finally, circumstances will begin to change and fall into harmony with your desires instead of being adverse to them.

Everyone knows how strong thoughts of fear or grief have turned hair white in a few hours; how great fear makes the heart beat so rapidly as to seem about to "jump out of the body," this result not being at all dependent upon whether there is any real cause for fear or it be a purely imaginary cause. Just so, strong thoughts of criticism will render the blood acid, causing rheumatism. Bearing mental burdens makes more stooped shoulders than does bearing heavy material loads. Believing that God regards us as "miserable sinners," that he is continually watching us and our failures with disapproval, brings utter discouragement and a sort of half-paralyzed condition of mind and body, which mean failure in all our undertakings.

Is it difficult for you to understand why, if God lives in us all the time, he does not keep our thoughts right instead of permitting us through ignorance to drift into wrong thoughts, and so bring trouble upon ourselves?

Well, we are not automatons. Your child will never learn to walk alone if you always do his walking. Because you recognize that the only way for him to be strong, self-reliant in all things—in other words, to become a man—is to throw him upon himself, and let him through *experience* come to a knowledge of things for himself, you are not willing to make a mere puppet of him by taking the steps for him, even though you know he will fall down many

a time and give himself severe bumps in the ongoing
toward perfect physical manhood.

We are in process of growth into the highest spiritual manhood and womanhood. We do get many
a fall and bump on the way, but only through these,
not necessarily *by* them, can our growth proceed.
No father, no mother, no matter how strong or deep
their love, can grow for their children. Nor can
God, who is omnipotence, at the center of our being,
grow spiritually for us without making of us automatons instead of individuals.

If you keep your thoughts turned toward the external of yourself, or of others, you will see only
the things which are not real, but temporal, and
which pass away. All the faults, failures or lacks
in people or circumstances will seem very real to you,
and you will be unhappy, miserable and sick.

If you turn your thoughts away from the external toward the spiritual, and let them dwell on the
good in yourself and others, all the apparent evil will
first drop out of your thoughts and then out of your
life. Paul understood this when he wrote the Phil-
ippians: "Finally, brethren, whatsoever things are
true, whatsoever things are honest, whatsoever things
are just, whatsoever things are pure, whatsoever
things are lovely, whatsoever things are of good re-

port; if there be any virtue, and if there be any
praise, think on *these* things."

We can each learn how to turn our conscious
mind toward the Universal Mind, or the Spirit within
us. We can, by practice, learn how to make this
everyday, topsy-turvy, carnal mind be still—actually
to stop thinking—and the Mind which is God (all
Wisdom, all Love) think in us and out through us.

Imagine, if you will, a great reservoir, out of
which lead innumerable small rivulets or channels.
At its farther end each channel opens out into a
small fountain. This fountain is not only being continually filled and replenished from the reservoir,
but is itself a radiating center from whence it gives
out in all directions that which it receives, so that all
who come within its radius are refreshed and blessed.

That is exactly our relation to God. Each one
of us is a radiating center. Each one, no matter how
small or ignorant, is the little fountain at the far
end of the channel, the other end of which opens out
in all there is in God. This fountain represents
our free will, or individuality, as separate from the
Great Reservoir—God—and yet as one with him
in that we are constantly fed and renewed from him;
and that without him we are nothing.

Each one of us, no matter how insignificant we

may be to the world, may receive from God unlimited good of whatever kind we desire, and radiate it to all around us. But remember, we must *radiate* if we would receive more. Stagnation is death.

Oh, I want the simplest mind to grasp this idea that the very wisdom of God, the love, the life, the power, which is God, is ready and waiting with longing impulse to flow out through us in unlimited degree! When it flows in unusual degree through these intellects, men exclaim, "What a wonderful mind!" when through these hearts, it is the love which melts all bitterness, envy, selfishness, jealousy, before it; when through our bodies as life, no disease can withstand its onward march.

We do not have to beseech God any more than we have to beseech the sun to shine. The sun shines because it is a law of its being to shine, and it cannot help it. No more can God help pouring into us unlimited wisdom, life, power, all good, because to give is a law of his being. Nothing can hinder him except our own free will. The sun may shine ever so brightly, but if we have through willfulness or ignorance placed ourselves, or been placed by our progenitors in the far corner of a damp, dark cellar, we do not get either joy or comfort from its shining; then to us the sun never shines.

So we have heretofore known nothing of how to get ourselves out of the cellar of ignorance, doubt and despair; and to our wrong thinking God has seemed to withhold the life, wisdom, power, we wanted so much, though we besought him never so earnestly.

The sun does not radiate life and warmth today and darkness and chill tomorrow; it cannot from the nature of its being. Nor does God radiate love at one time, while at others, anger, wrath and displeasure flow out from his mind toward us.

"Doth a fountain send forth at the same place sweet water and bitter? Can a fig tree, my brethren, bear olive berries? either a vine figs?"

God is All-Good—always good, always love. He never changes, no matter what we do or may have done. He is always trying to pour more of himself through us into visibility so as to make us grander, larger, fuller, freer individuals.

While the child is crying out for its Father-Mother God, the Father-Mother is yearning with infinite tenderness to satisfy the child.

> "In the heart of man a cry,
> In the heart of God supply."

RECAPITULATION

There is but One Mind in the universe.

Mortal mind is false mind, or intellect. It gathers its information and speaks from *without*.

Universal Mind sees and speaks from *within*.

Our ways of thinking make our happiness or unhappiness, our success or non-success. We can by effort change our ways of thinking.

God is at all times, regardless of our so-called sins, trying to pour more good into our lives to make them larger and more successful.

DENIALS

Then said Jesus unto his disciples, If any man will come after me, let him deny himself, and take up his cross, and follow me.—*Matt. 16:24.*

All systems for spiritualizing the mind include much denial. Every religion in all the ages had some sort of denial as one of its foundations. We all know how the Puritans believed that the more rigidly they denied themselves any comfort the better they pleased God. So far has this idea taken possession of the human mind during some ages that devout souls have even tortured their bodies in various ways, believing that they were thus making themselves more spiritual, or at least were in some way placating an angry God. Even today most people interpret the above saying of Jesus as meaning, If any man wants to please God he must give up about all the enjoyment and comfort he has, all things he likes and wants, and must take up the heavy cross of constantly doing the things which are repugnant to him in his daily life. This is why many young people say, "When I am old I will be a Christian, but not now, for I want to enjoy life a while first."

There could, I am sure, be nothing further from the meaning of the Nazarene than the above interpretation. In our ignorance of the nature of God, our Father, and of our relation to him, we have believed that all our enjoyment came from external sources, usually from gaining possession of something we did not have. The poor see enjoyment only in possessing abundance of money. The rich, who are satiated with life's so-called pleasures until their lives have become like a person with an overloaded stomach compelled to sit constantly at a well-spread table, are often the most bitter in the complaint that life holds no happiness for them. The sick one believes that were he well he would be perfectly happy. The healthy but hard-working man or woman feels the need of some days of rest and recreation that the monotony of his or her life may be broken.

So ever the mind has been turned to some external change of condition or circumstance in pursuit of satisfaction and enjoyment. In after years, when men have tried all, getting first this thing and then that, which they thought would yield them happiness, and have been grievously disappointed, they in a kind of desperation turn to God and try to find some sort of comfort in believing that sometime, somewhere, they will get what they want and be happy. Thenceforth their lives are patient and submissive, but they are destitute of any real joy.

This same Nazarene, to whom we always go back because to us he is the best-known teacher and demonstrator of truth, spent nearly three years teaching the people—the common everyday people like you and me, who wanted, just as we do, food and rent and clothing, money, friends and love—to love their enemies, and do good to those who persecuted them; to resist not evil in any way, but to give double to any one who tried to get away what belonged to them; to cease from all anxiety regarding the things they needed, because "your heavenly Father knoweth that ye have need of all these things." And then in talking one day he said, "These things have I spoken unto you, that my joy might remain in you, and that your joy might be full." And another day he said, "Whatsoever ye shall ask of the Father in my name, he will give it you." "Ask and ye shall receive, that your joy may be full." And again, "I do not say that I will entreat the Father for you, for the Father himself loves you." We have further learned that God is the sum total of all the good in the universe, and that there is in the Mind which is God a perpetual desire to pour more of himself—the substance of all good things— through us into visibility, or into our lives.

Surely all these things do not look as though, when Jesus said that the way to be like him and possess like power, was to *deny* yourself, he meant that we are to go without the enjoyable comforts of life, or in any way deprive or torture ourselves.

In these lessons we have seen that besides the real innermost Self of each of us—the Self spelled with a capital "S," because it is an expression or pressing out of God into visibility, and is always one with the Father—there is a *mortal self*, a carnal mind, which reports lies from the external world, and is not to be relied upon at all; this is the self of which Jesus spoke when he said, "Deny yourself." This intellect man, carnal mind, mortal mind, or whatever you choose to call him, is envious and jealous and fretful and sick because he is *selfish*. This mortal self is always seeking its own gratification at the expense, if need be, of some one else.

The Self of you is never sick, never afraid, never selfish. It is the part of every man which "seeketh not his own, is not puffed up, thinketh no evil." It is always seeking to give to others, while the self

is always seeking her own. Heretofore we have
lived in the self region. We have believed all that
this false mind has told us, and the consequence is
we have been overwhelmed with all kinds of pri-
vation and suffering.

Some people, who, during the last few years,
have been making a special study of the mind, find
it a fact that certain wrong or false beliefs held by
us are really the cause of all sorts of trouble—physical, moral and financial. They have learned that
wrong (or, as they call them, *error*) beliefs arise
only in the carnal or mortal mind; and they have
learned *and actually proven* that we can by a per-
sistent effort of the will change our beliefs, and by
this means alone entirely change our troublesome
circumstances and bodily conditions.

One of the methods which they have found will
work every time in getting rid of troublesome conditions (which are all the result of believing the lies
told us by the carnal mind, the senses) is to deny
them *in toto*: first, to deny that any such things have
or could have power to make us unhappy; second,
to deny that these things do in reality exist at all.

The word "deny" has two definitions, according
to Webster. To deny, in one sense, is to *withhold
from*, as to deny bread to the hungry. To deny, in

another sense (and we believe it was in this latter way that Jesus used it), is *to declare not to be true, to repudiate as utterly false.* To deny one's self, then, is not to withhold comfort or happiness from the external man, much less to inflict torture upon it, but it is *to deny the claims of this false self* called "mortal mind"—to declare these claims to be untrue.

If you have done any piece of work wrong, the very first step toward getting it right is to undo the wrong, to erase from the slate so far as possible the wrong figures you have made, and begin again from the foundation. We have believed wrong about God and about ourselves. We have believed that God was angry with us, and that we were, at the best, great sinners who ought to be (and most of us are) afraid of him. We believed that sickness and poverty and trouble were evil things put here by this same God just to torture us in some way into serving him and loving him. We have believed that we have pleased God best when we became so absolutely paralyzed by our troubles as to be patiently submissive to them all, and not even try to rise out of them or overcome them. All false, entirely false! And the first step toward freeing ourselves from our

troubles is to get rid of our erroneous beliefs about
God and about ourselves.

"But," objects one, "if a thing is not so, and I
have believed a lie about it, I do not see just how
my believing wrong about it could affect my bodily
health or my circumstances."

A child can be so afraid of an imaginary bugaboo under the bed as to have convulsions or become
insane. Should you today receive a telegraphic message that your husband, wife or child, who is away
from you, had been suddenly killed, your suffering,
mental and physical, and perhaps extending even to
your external and financial affairs, would be just as
great as though it were really true; and yet the report may have been entirely false. Exactly so have
these messages of bugaboos behind the doors, bugaboos of divine wrath and of our own weakness, come
to us through the senses until we are paralyzed by
our fears of them.

Now let us arouse ourselves. Denial is the first
practical step toward wiping out of our minds the
mistaken beliefs of a lifetime—the beliefs which
have made such sad havoc in our lives. By denial
we mean declaring a thing which *seems* true *not* to
be true. Appearances are directly opposed to the
teachings of truth or science. Jesus said, "Judge

not according to the appearance, but judge righteous [right] judgment."

Suppose you had always been taught that the sun really moved or revolved around the earth, and some one should now try to persuade you that the opposite was the truth. You would see at a glance that such might be the case, and yet as often as you saw the sun rise, the old impression, made on your mind by the wrong belief of years, would come up and seem almost too real to be disputed. The only way you could cleanse your mind of the impression, and make the untrue seem unreal, would be by repeatedly denying the old belief; saying over and over to yourself as often as the subject came up in your mind, "This is not true, the sun does not move; it stands still, and the earth moves." Eventually the sun would not even *seem* to move.

The appearances are that our bodies and our circumstances control our thoughts, but science says directly the reverse.

If you repeatedly deny a false or unhappy condition, it not only loses its power to make you unhappy, but eventually the condition itself is destroyed by your denial.

What every one desires is to have only the good manifested in his life and surroundings—to have his

life full of love, to have perfect health, to know all
things, to have great power and much joy; *and this
is just exactly what God wants us to have.* All love
is God in manifestation, as we have learned in a
previous lesson. All wisdom is God. All life and
health is God. All joy (because all good) and all
power are God. All good of whatever kind is God
come forth into visibility through people or some
other visible form. When we crave more of any
good thing, we are in reality craving more of God
to come forth into our lives so that we can *realize* it
by the senses. Having more of God does not take
out of our lives the good things—*it only puts more
of them in.* In the mind, which is God, there is
always the desire to give more, for the divine impulse is forever to get more of itself into visibility.

Intellectually we may see the fact of our own
God-being which never changes. What we need is
to *realize* our oneness with the Father at all times.
In order to realize it we *deny the appearances in
ourselves and others which seem contrary to this—
deny them as realities;* declare they are not true.

There are four or five great error thoughts which
nearly every one holds, and which the people who
have grown out of sickness and trouble by these
means have found it good for all people to deny in

order to cleanse the mind of the direful effects of believing them. They are something like this:

First, There is no evil.

There is but one power in the universe, and that is God—Good. God is all good, and God is omni-present. Apparent evils are not entities or things of themselves. They are simply an absence of the good, just as darkness is an absence of light. But God, or Good, is omnipresent, so the apparent ab-sence of good (evil) is unreal. It is only an *appear-ance* of evil, just as the moving sun was an appear-ance. You need not wait to discuss this matter of evil or to fully understand all about why you deny it, but just begin to practice the denials in an unprej-udiced way and see how marvelously it will, after a little, deliver you from some of the so-called evils of your daily life.

Second, There is no absence of life, substance or intelligence anywhere.

We have seen that the real is the spiritual. "The things which are seen are temporal; but the things which are not seen are eternal." By using this denial you will soon break the bondage you are in to matter and to material conditions. You will know you are free.

Third, Pain, sickness, poverty, old age, death, cannot master me, for they are not real.

Fourth, There is nothing in all the universe for me to fear, for greater is He that is within me than he that is in the world.

God says, "I will contend with him that contendeth with thee." He says it to every living child of his, and every person is his child.

Repeat these four denials silently several times a day, not with a strained anxiety to get something out of them, but trying calmly to realize the meaning of the words spoken:

There is no evil (or devil).

There is no reality, life or intelligence apart from Spirit.

Pain, sickness, poverty, old age and death are not real, and they have no power over me.

There is nothing in all the universe for me to fear.

Almost hourly little vexations and fears come up in your life. Meet each one with a denial. Calmly and coolly say within yourself, "That's nothing at all. It cannot harm or disturb me or make me unhappy." Do not vigorously fight it, but let your denial be the denial of superiority to it, as you would deny the power of ants on their little hill to disturb you. If you are angry, stand still, and silently deny

it. Say you are not angry; you are love made
manifest, and cannot be angry; it is not true, etc.,
and the anger will suddenly leave you entirely.

If some one shows you ill-will, silently deny his
power to hurt you or make you unhappy. Should
you find yourself feeling jealous or envious towards
any one, instantly turn the heel of negation on the
hydra-headed monster. Declare you are not jealous; that you are an expression of Perfect Love
(which expression is God pressed out into visibility),
and cannot feel jealousy. There is really nothing
and no one to be jealous of, for all people are one
and the same Spirit. "And there are diversities of
operations [or manifestations], but it is the *same
God* which worketh in all," says St. Paul. How
can you be jealous of another part of yourself which
seems to you "more comely"?

Shall the foot be jealous of the hand, or the ear
of the eye? Are not the seemingly feeble members
of the body just as important to the perfection of the
whole as the others? Do you seem to be less or
have less than some others? Remember that all envy
and jealousy is in the false or mortal mind, and that
in reality you, however insignificant, are an *absolute
necessity* to God in order to make the perfect whole.

If you find yourself dreading to meet any one, or

afraid to step out and do what you want or ought to do, immediately begin to say, "It is not true; I am not afraid; I am Perfect Love, and can know no fear. No one, nothing in all the universe, can hurt me." You will find after a little that all the fear has disappeared, all trepidation is gone.

Denials bring freedom from bondage, and happiness comes when we can effectually deny the power of things to touch or trouble us.

Have you been living in the negations for years, denying your ability to succeed, denying your health, denying your Godhood, denying your power to accomplish anything, by feeling yourself a child of the devil or of weakness? If so, this constant negation has paralyzed you and destroyed your power.

When, in the next lesson, you learn something about affirmations—the opposite of negations—you will know how to lift yourself out of the realm of failure into that of success.

All your happiness, all your health and power, come from God. They flow in an unbroken stream from the Fountainhead into the very center of your being, and radiate from center to circumference, or to the senses. When you acknowledge this constantly, and deny that outside things can hinder your happiness or health or power, it helps the sense nature to *realize* health and power and happiness.

No person or thing in the universe, no chain of circumstances, can by any possibility interpose itself between you and all joy—all good. You may falsely *think* that something stands between you and your heart's desire, and so live with that desire unfulfilled; but it is not true. This "think" is the bugaboo under the bed that has no reality. Deny it, deny it, and you will find yourself free, and you will realize that this seeming was all false. Good will then begin to flow in to you, and you will see clearly that nothing can stand between you and your own.

Denials should be spoken silently and audibly, but not in a manner to call forth antagonism and discussion.

To some all this sort of mechanical working will seem a strange way of entering into a more spiritual life. There are those who easily and naturally glide out of the old material life into a deeper spiritual one without any external helps. But there are also thousands of people hungering today for a higher life, and thousands of others who are seeking primarily the loaves and fishes of bodily health and financial success, but really are just the same seeking a higher life, who must needs take the very first steps. For such, practicing these mechanical rules in a whole-hearted way, without prejudice, is doing the very best thing possible towards purity of heart and life, towards growth in divine knowledge, and fullness of joy in all things undertaken.

AFFIRMATIONS

FOURTH LESSON

Thou shalt make thy prayer unto him, and he shall hear thee, and thou shalt pay thy vows. Thou shalt also decree a thing and it shall be established unto thee; and the light shall shine upon thy ways.—*Job 22:27, 28.*

Most people, when they first consciously set out to gain a fuller, higher knowledge of spiritual things, do so because of dissatisfaction—or perhaps unsatisfaction would be the better word—with their past and present condition of life. Inherent in the human mind is the thought that somewhere, somehow, it ought to be able to bring to itself that which it desires and which would satisfy. This thought is but the foreshadowing of that which really is.

> "Our wishes, it is said, do measure just
> Our capabilities. Who with his might
> Aspires unto the mountain's upper height,
> Holds in that aspiration a great trust
> To be fulfilled, a warrant that he must
> Not disregard, a strength to reach the height
> To which his hopes have taken flight."

The hunger we feel is but the prompting of the Divine within us, which longs with an infinite longing to fill us. It is but one side of the law of demand and supply, the other side of which is unchangeably, unfailingly, the promise, "What things soever ye desire, when ye pray, believe that ye receive them, and ye shall have them." The supply is always equal to the demand, but there must first be a demand before supply is of use.

There is a place attainable by us where we see that our doing can cease, because Spirit is the fulfillment of all our desires. We simply "be still and know" that all things whatsoever we desire are ours already; and this knowing it, or recognizing it, has power to bring the invisible God (or Good), who is the innermost *substance* of all things, forth into just the visible form of good we want.

But in order to attain this place of power we must take the preliminary steps, faithfully, earnestly, trustingly, though these steps at first glance seem to us as useless and ridiculous as do the ceremonial forms and religious observances of the ritualistic churchman.

To affirm anything is to assert positively, even in the face of all contrary evidence, that it is so. We may not be able to see *how*, by our simply affirming a thing to be true, which to all human reasoning or sight does not seem to be true at all, we can bring that thing to pass; but we can compel ourselves to cease all quibbling and go to work to prove the rule each one for himself.

This beautiful Presence all about us and within us is the substance of every good which we can possibly desire—aye, infinitely more than we are capable of desiring; for "Eye hath not seen, nor ear heard, neither have entered into the heart of man, the things which God hath prepared for them that love him."

In some way, which it is not easy to put into words—for spiritual laws cannot always be compassed in mortal words, and yet they are none the less infallible, immutable laws which work with precision and certainty—there is power in our *word of faith* to bring all good things right into our everyday life.

We speak the word, we confidently affirm, but we have nothing to do with the "establishing" of the word, or the bringing it to pass. "Thou shalt also decree a thing, and *it shall be established unto thee*," it says. If we decree or affirm unwaveringly, steadfastly, we hold God by his own unalterable laws to do the establishing or fulfilling.

They who have carefully studied spiritual laws find that besides denying the reality and power of apparent evil, which denying frees them from it, they also can bring any desired good into their lives by persistently affirming it is there already. In the first instructions given to students, the denials and affirmations take a large place. Later on, their own personal experiences and inward guidance lead them up to a higher plane where they no longer need rules.

The saying over of any denial or affirmation is a necessary self-training of mind which has lived so long in error and false beliefs that it needs this constant repetition of truth to unclothe it and clothe it anew.

As it is with the denials, so with the affirmations. There are four or five great sweeping affirmations of truth which cover a multitude of lesser ones, and which do marvelous work in bringing good to ourselves and to others:

First, God is Life, Love, Intelligence, Substance, Omnipotence, Omniscience, Omnipresence.

This you will remember from the first lesson—the Statement of Being. As you repeat the affirmation please remember that every particle of life, of love, intelligence, power, or of real substance in the universe is simply a certain degree, or, so to speak, *quality* of God made manifest or visible through a

form. Try to think what is meant when you say
God is omnipresent, omnipotent, omniscient.

If God is omnipresent (all presence), and is all
good, where is the evil? If he is omnipotence (all
power), what other power can there be working in
the universe?

Since God is Omnipotence and Omnipresence,
put aside forever your traditional teaching of an adverse power, evil (devil), that may at any moment
thwart the plans of Good and bring you harm.

Do not disturb yourself about the *appearances*
of evil all about you; but in the very presence of
what seems evil stand true and unwavering in affirming God, the Good, is omnipresent, or *all* there is
present. By so doing you will see the seeming evil
all melt away as the darkness before the light or the
dew before the morning sun, and good come to take
its place.

Second, I am a child or manifestation of God,
and every moment his life, love, wisdom, power flow
into and through me. I am one with God, and am
governed by his laws.

Remember while repeating this affirmation that
nothing—no circumstance, no person or set of persons—can by any possibility interpose between you
and the Source of your life, wisdom or power. It

is all "hid with Christ [the innermost Christ or Spirit of your being] in God." Nothing but your own ignorance of how to receive, or your willfulness, can hinder you having unlimited supply.

No matter how sick or weak or inefficient you seem to be, take your eyes and thoughts right off the seeming and turn them within to the Central Fountain there, and say calmly, quietly, but with steadfast assurance, "This appearance of weakness is false; the life, the wisdom, the power, which is God, is now flowing into my entire being and out through me to the external," and you will soon see a marvelous change wrought in you by the realization this spoken word will bring to you.

You do not change God's attitude towards you one iota, by either importuning or affirming. You only change your attitude towards him who is *always* on the giving hand. By thus affirming you put yourself into harmony with the divine law, which is always working towards your good and never towards your harm or punishment.

Third, I am Spirit, perfect, holy, harmonious. Nothing can hurt me or make me sick or afraid, for Spirit is God, and cannot be hurt or made sick or afraid. I manifest my real Self through this body now.

Fourth, God works in me to will and to do whatsoever he wishes me to do, and he cannot fail.

Affirming his mind working both to will and to do makes us will only the good; and he, the very Father in us, doeth the works, hence there can be no failure. Whatsoever we fully commit to the Father to do, and affirm is done, we shall see accomplished. These, then, are the four comprehensive affirmations:

First, God is Life, Love, Intelligence, Substance, Omnipotence, Omnipresence, Omniscience.

Second, I am the child or manifestation of God; and his life, love wisdom, power, flow into and through me every moment. I am one with God, and am governed by his law.

Third, I am Spirit, perfect, holy, harmonious. Nothing can hurt me or make me sick or afraid, for Spirit is God, and God cannot be sick or hurt or afraid. I manifest my real Self now.

Fourth, God works in me to will and to do whatsoever he wishes done by me; hence I cannot fail.

Commit each one of these affirmations to memory, so that you may repeat them in the silence of your own mind in any place and at any time. Strangely will they act to deliver you out of the greatest external distresses, places where no human

help avails.   It is as though the moment you assert
emphatically your oneness with God the Father,
there is instantly set in motion all the power of omnipotent love to rush to your rescue.   And when *it*
has undertaken for you, you can cease from external
ways and means, and boldly claim, "It is done; I
have the desires of my heart."   "Thou openest thine
hand, and satisfiest the desire of every living thing,"
said the Psalmist.

In reality God is forever in process of movement
toward us that he may manifest more fully himself
(all good) through us.   Our affirming, backed by
faith, is the grip which connects the car of your conscious human need with the ever-moving cable of his
power and supply.

They who have claimed their birthright by thus
calmly affirming their oneness with God, know how
still they can be from external planning and efforts
after they have called into operation this marvelous
power by affirmation.   It has healed the sick,
brought joy in place of mourning, literally opened
prison doors and bid the prisoner go free, without
one particle of human effort or assistance.

Understand, it is not necessarily using just this
form of words that has availed in each individual
case; but it has been the denying of apparent evil,

and in spite of all contrary evidence affirming the
good to be all there is; affirming our oneness with
God's omnipotent power to accomplish, even when
there were no visible signs of his being present, that
wrought the deliverance. In one case within my
knowledge, just simply claiming, "God is your defense and deliverance," for a man who had been
five years an exile from home and country through a
series of deceptions and machinations which for
depth and subtlety were unparalleled, opened all the
doors wide and restored the man to his family within
a month, without one single effort or step taken from
the human side; and that, too, after five years of the
most strenuous human efforts of lawyers, etc., having
failed utterly to bring the truth to light or to release
the prisoner.

Some minds are so constituted as to get better
results from repeated use of denials; others from
using denials less and affirmations more.

No definite rules can be laid down as to which
will work most effectually in each individual case
to eradicate apparent evil and bring into manifestation the good. But some little hint can be given
which may be helpful.

Denials have an erasive or destructive tendency.
Affirmations build up, and give strength and cour-

age and power. People who remember vividly, and are inclined to dwell in their thoughts on the pains, sorrows and troubles of the past or present, need to deny a great deal; for denials cleanse the mind and blot out of memory all seeming evils and unhappiness, so that they become as a far-away dream. Again, denials are particularly useful to those who are hard or intolerant, or aggressively sinful; to those who, as a result of success, have become over-confident, thinking the mortal is sufficient of itself for all things; to the selfish, and to any who do not scruple to harm others.

Affirmations should be used by the timid and those who have a feeling of their own inefficiency; those who stand in fear of other minds; those who "give in" easily; those who are subject to anxiety or doubt, and those who are in positions of responsibility. The people who are in any way negative or passive need to use affirmations more; the ones who are self-confident or unforgiving, need denials more. Deny evil; affirm good. Deny weakness; affirm strength. Deny any undesirable condition, and affirm the good you desire. This is what Jesus meant when he said, "What things soever ye desire, when ye pray, believe [or claim or affirm] that ye receive them, and ye shall have them" (Mark 11:24). It is what is meant by the promise, "Every place that the sole of your foot shall tread upon [or that you stand squarely and firmly upon], that have I given you."

Practice these denials and affirmations silently on the street, in the cars, when you are wakeful during the night, anywhere, everywhere, and it will give you a new, and, to you, strange mastery over external things and over yourself. If there comes a moment when you are in doubt as to what to do, stand still and affirm, "God *in me* is Infinite Wisdom; I know just what to do." "For I will give you a mouth and wisdom, which all your adversaries shall not be able to gainsay nor resist." Do not get flustered nor anxious, but depend fully and trustingly on your principle, and you will be surprised at the sudden inspiration which will come to you as to the mode of procedure.

So *always* this principle will work in the solution of all life's problems—I care not what the form of detail is—to free us, God's children, from all undesirable conditions, and to bring good into our lives, if we will take up the simple rules and use them faithfully, until they lead us into such realization of our Godhood that we need no longer depend upon them.

FAITH

FIFTH LESSON

For verily I say unto you, That whosoever shall say unto this mountain, Be thou removed, and be thou cast into the sea; and shall not doubt in his heart, but shall believe that those things which he saith shall come to pass; he shall have whatsoever he saith.—*Mark 11:23*.

Science was Faith once.—*Lowell.*

The word "faith" is one which has generally been thought to denote a simple form of belief based mostly upon ignorance and superstition. It is a word that has drawn forth something akin to scorn from so-called "thinking people"—the people who have believed that intellectual attainment was the highest form of knowledge to be reached. "Blind faith" they have disdainfully chosen to call it—fit only for ministers, women and children, but not a practical thing upon which to establish the everyday business affairs of life.

Some have prided themselves on having outgrown the swaddling clothes of this blind, unreasoning faith, and grown up to the place, as they say, where they have faith only in that which can be seen and handled, or intellectually explained.

54

St. Paul, a most intellectual man, and a learned theologian, after having written at length upon the nature of faith and the marvelous results attending it, tried to put into a few words a condensed definition of faith:

"Faith is the substance of things hoped for, the evidence of things not seen," said he.—Heb. 11:1.

In other words, faith takes right hold of the substance of the things desired, and brings into the world of evidence the things which before were not seen. Further speaking of faith, Paul says: "Things which are seen were not made of things which do appear;" *i. e.*, things which are seen are not made out of visible things, but out of the invisible. In some way, then, we understand that whatever we want is in this surrounding invisible Substance, and faith is the power which can bring it out into reality to us. Please remember this.

After having related innumerable instances of marvelous things brought to pass in the lives of men, not by their work or efforts, but by faith, Paul says:

"And what shall I more say? for the time would fail me to tell of Gedeon, and of Barak, and of Samson, and of Jephthæ; of David also, and Samuel, and of the prophets:

"Who through faith subdued kingdoms, wrought righteousness, obtained promises, stopped the mouths of lions,

"Quenched the violence of fire, escaped the edge of

the sword, out of the weakness were made strong, waxed
valiant in fight, turned to flight the armies of the aliens.

"Women received their dead to life again," etc.—
Hebrews 11:32-35.

Is there any more power or anything greater you
want in your life than is here mentioned by Paul?
Power to subdue kingdoms, to stop the mouths of
lions, quench fire, turn to flight whole armies, raise
your dead to life again? Even if your desires ex-
ceed this, you need not despair or hesitate to claim
their fulfillment, for One greater than I, One who
knew whereof he spoke, said, "To him that be-
lieveth, *all* things are possible."

Until very recently, whenever any one has spoken of faith as the one power which could move
mountains (or move God, which was still more difficult), we have always felt a sort of hopeless discouragement. While we have believed that God
holds all good things in his hand, and is willing to be
prevailed upon to dole them out "according to your
faith," yet how could we, even by straining every
nerve of our being towards faith, be sure that we
have sufficient to please him? For does it not say,
"Without faith it is impossible to please God"?

From the moment we began to ask we began to
question our ability to reach God's standard of faith
upon which hung our fate. We also began to feel

rather shaky about whether, after all, there is any such power in faith to prevail with the Giver of every good gift as to draw out of him something which he had never let us have before.

Viewing faith in this light, it isn't much wonder that logical minds have looked upon it as a sort of will-o'-the-wisp, good enough for weak women and silly children to hang their hopes upon, but not a thing upon which any real, definite results could ever be counted—not a thing that the business world could rest upon.

There is a "blind faith," to be sure. (Some one has truthfully said that blind faith is better than none at all; for if held to, it will get its eyes open after a time.) But there is also an understanding faith. Blind faith is an instinctive trust in a power higher than ourselves. Understanding faith is based upon immutable principle.

Faith does not depend upon physical facts, or evidence of the senses, because it is born of intuition, or the Spirit of Truth ever living at the center of our being. Its action is infinitely higher than that of intellectual conclusions; it is founded on Truth.

Intuition is the open end, within one's own being, of the invisible channel ever connecting each individual with God. Faith is, as it were, a ray of light

shot out from the Central Sun—God—the farther
end of which ray comes into your being and mine
through the open door of intuition.   With our consciousness we *perceive* the ray of light, and though
intellect cannot grasp it, or give the why or wherefore thereof, yet we instinctively feel that the other
end of the ray opens out into all there is of God
(Good).   This is "blind" faith.   It is based on
truth, but a truth which we are not at the time conscious of.   Even this kind of faith will, if persisted
in, bring the desired results.

Now, what is understanding faith?   There are
some things which God has so indissolubly joined
together that it is impossible for even himself to put
them asunder.   They are bound together by fixed,
immutable laws.   If we have one, we must have the
other.

Evans illustrates this by the laws of geometry.
For instance, if we have a triangle, the sum of all
the angles is equal to two right angles.   No matter
how large or small the triangle, no matter whether
it is made on the mountain top or leagues under the
sea, if we are asked the sum of its angles we can un-
hesitatingly answer, without waiting an instant to
count or reckon this particular triangle, that it is
just two right angles.   This is absolutely certain.   It

is certain before even the triangle is drawn by visible lines; and we can know it beforehand, because it is based upon immutable, unchangeable laws, upon the truth or reality of the thing. It was true just as much before any one ever recognized it as it is today. People knowing it or not knowing it does not change the fact. *Only just in proportion as we come to know it as an eternally true fact can we be benefited by it.*

It is a simple fact that one plus one makes two; it is an eternal truth. You cannot put one and one together without the two resulting. You may believe it or not; that does not alter the fact. But unless you do put the one and one together you cannot produce the two, for one is eternally dependent upon the other.

There are in the mental and spiritual worlds, or realms, just as real and unfailing laws for their government as in the natural world. There are certain conditions of mind which are so connected with certain results that the two are inseparable. If we have the one, we must have the other, as surely as the night follows the day. Not because we believe some wise person's testimony that such is the case, not even because the voice of intuition tells us it is so,

but because the whole matter is based on laws which
can neither fail nor be broken.

When we know something of these laws, we can
know positively beforehand just what results will
follow certain mental states.

God, the one creative cause of all things, is
Spirit, and visible to spiritual consciousness, as we
have learned. God is the sum total of all good.
There is no good you can desire in your life but
what at its center it is God. God is the *Substance*
of all things—the real thing within every visible
form of good.

God, the invisible Substance out of which all
visible things are formed, is all around us waiting to
come forth into visible manifestation.

This Good Substance all about us is unlimited,
and is *itself the supply of every demand that can be
made; of every need that exists in the visible or natural world.*

One of the unerring truths or facts in the universe
(by "universe" I mean the spiritual and natural
worlds combined) is that *somewhere there is already
provided a lavish abundance for every human want.*
In other words, the supply of every good always
somewhere awaits the demand. Another truth, or
fact, is that the demand must be made before the

supply can come forth to fill it. To recognize these two statements of truth, and to affirm them, is the whole secret of understanding faith—faith based on principle or understanding.

Let us square this by Paul's definition of faith, given earlier in the lesson, "Faith is the substance of things hoped for, the evidence of things not seen." Faith takes hold of the substance of the thing hoped for, and brings into evidence, or visibility, the things not seen.

What are usually called the promises of God are certain eternal, unchangeable truths, that are true whether they are found in the Bible or the almanac. They are the unvarying statement of *facts* which cannot be altered. A promise, according to Webster, is something sent beforehand to indicate that something unseen is at hand. It is a declaration which gives the person to whom it is made the right to expect and claim the performance of the act.

When the Nazarene, who had recognized the unchangeable fact that the supply of every want awaited, in the unseen, the demand for it, said, "If ye ask, ye receive," he was simply stating an unalterable truth. He had learned enough of spiritual law to know that the instant we ask or desire (for asking is desire expressed) we touch a secret spring which starts the good we want on its way towards us. He knew that there need not be any coaxing or pleading about it; that our asking was simply complying with an unfailing law which was *bound* to work; there was no escape from it. Asking and receiving are the two ends of one and the same thing. We cannot have one without the other.

Asking springs from desire to possess some good. What is desire? *Desire in the heart is always God tapping at the door of your consciousness with his infinite supply*—a supply which is forever useless unless there be demand for it. "Before they call, I will answer" (Isaiah 65:24). Before ever you are conscious of any lack, of any desire for more happiness, for fullness of joy, the great Father-Mother heart has desired them for you. It is he desiring them *in* you that you feel, and think it is only yourself (separate from him) desiring them. With God the desire to give and giving are one and the same thing. Evans says, "Desire for anything is the thing itself in incipiency;" *i. e.*, the thing you desire is not only for you, but has already been started towards you out of the heart of God; and *it is the first little approach of the thing itself striking you* that makes you desire it, or even think of it at all.

The only way God has of letting us know of his

infinite supply, and his desire to make it ours, is for
him to gently push upon this little divine spark living
within each one of us. He wants you to be a strong,
self-efficient man or woman, to have more power and
dominion over all before you; so he quietly and silently pushes a little more of himself, his desire, into
the center of your being. He enlarges, so to speak,
your real Self, and at once you become conscious of
new desire to be bigger, grander, stronger. If he
had not pushed at the center of your being first, you
would never have thought of it, but would have remained perfectly content as you were.

You think you want better health, more love, a
brighter, more cheerful home all your very own; in
short, you want less evil (or no evil) and more good
in your life. This is only God pushing at the inner
door of your being, saying, "My child, let me in; I
want to give you *all* good, that you may be more
comfortable and happy." "Behold, my servants
shall eat; behold, my servants shall drink; behold,
my servants shall build houses and inhabit them; behold, my servants shall rejoice and sing for joy of
heart."

Remember this: *Desire in the heart for anything is God's sure promise sent beforehand to indicate that it is yours already* in the limitless realm of

supply; and whatever you want, you can have for the taking.

Taking is simply recognizing the law of supply and demand (even if you cannot see with this mortal understanding a sign of the supply any more than Elijah did when he had affirmed for rain, and not a cloud even so big as a man's hand was for a long time to be seen). Affirm your possession of the good you desire; have faith in it, because you are working on law and cannot fail; do not be argued off your basic principle by any one; and sooner will the heavens fall than that you fail to get that which you desire.

"All things whatsoever ye pray and ask for, believe that ye receive them, and ye shall have them." —Mark 11:24, R. V.

Knowing the law of abundant supply, and the fact that supply always precedes the demand, demand simply being the call which brings the supply into sight; knowing that all desire in the heart for any good is really God's desire *in* us and for us, how shall we obtain the fulfillment of our every desire, and that right speedily?

"Delight thyself in the Lord; and he shall give thee the desire of thine heart" (Psa. 37:4). Take right hold of God with an unwavering faith. Begin and continue to rejoice and thank him that you *have* (not will have) the desires of your heart, never losing sight of the fact that the *desire is the thing itself in incipiency.* If the good were not already yours in the invisible realm of supply, you could not by any possibility desire it.

One asks, "Suppose I desire my neighbor's wife, or his property; is that desire born of God? And can I see it fulfilled by affirming that it is mine?"

You do not and cannot by any possibility desire that which *belongs* to another. You do not desire your neighbor's wife. You desire the love which seems to you to be represented by your neighbor's wife. You desire something to fill your heart, craving for love. Affirm that there is for you a rightful and an overflowing supply, and claim its manifestation. It will surely come, and your desire (?) to possess your neighbor's wife will suddenly disappear.

So you do not in reality desire anything which belongs to your neighbor. You want the equivalent of that for which his possessions stand. *You want your own.* There is today an unlimited supply of all good provided in the unseen for every human being. No man must needs have less that another may have more. Your very own awaits you. Your understanding faith and trust is the power which will bring it to you.

As Emerson says, "The man who knows the law is sure that his welfare is dear to the heart of Being; he believes that he cannot escape from his good."

Knowing the divine law, we can forever rest from all anxiety, all fear, for "He openeth his hand, and satisfieth the desire of every living creature."

DEFINITION OF TERMS USED IN METAPHYSICAL TEACHINGS

SIXTH LESSON

One of the greatest beauties of the Sermon on the Mount is the perfectly childlike simplicity of its language. Every child and every grown person, be they ever so illiterate, if they can read at all, can understand it. Not a word in it requires the use of a dictionary; not a sentence in it but that tells the way so plainly that a "wayfarer though a fool may not err therein." And yet the Nazarene was the fullest, most complete manifestation of the One Mind that ever lived; that is to say, more of the wisdom, which is God, came forth through him into visibility than through any one else who ever lived. So it has always been. The more any person manifests the true wisdom, which is God, the more simple are his ways of thinking and acting; the more simple are the words through which he expresses his ideas. The greater the truth to be expressed, the more simply can it (and should it) be clothed.

Emerson said, "Converse with a mind that is grandly simple, and all literature [high-sounding

sentences to convey ideas] looks like mere word
catching."

In the metaphysical literature of today a good
many terms are used which are very confusing to
those who have not taken a consecutive course of
lessons on the subject. It seems to me wise to give
just here a clear, simple explanation of certain words
frequently used, so that even the most unlearned may
read understandingly.

You will often see the words, "Thought transference." This simply means the sending of thought
from one person's mind to another without using
either written or audible spoken words. There was
a time when, in order to communicate with any one
not in our presence, our thoughts must be laboriously
written down on paper and carried from one to another. Then, in the progress of things, came a time
when the Spirit within a certain man revealed to the
intellect of that man that a subtle fluid which was
not tangible, could neither be seen nor handled,
called "electricity," could be used to convey a message from point to point if it only had a connecting
wire between the two points on which to run, with
proper batteries at each end of the wire to keep up
the supply of electricity.

More recently, scientific people are learning that

they can dispense with the batteries and the connecting wire between two points, and can so project the silent thought of their own minds out through space to another mind, that the latter can inwardly hear or receive the message; as we say, the other mind "catches the thought." It is a sort of mental telegraphy, and is called "telepathy."

You have no moral right to use the power of thought transference in order to cause any one to carry out any plan which you may make for that one. You may think your neighbor rich, and may silently send him thoughts to give something to some good cause in which you are interested, or to some poor person, justifying yourself by saying, "That is not selfish; I do not want him to give to me, and it must be right for me to help others." You may feel justified in silently sending your thought into another one's mind to cause him to go to prayer meeting, or some other good place, because you desire him to lead a moral, upright life. Beware how you use this power of thought transference on your neighbor for any such specific purpose, though it may seem to your mortal mind as though the thing you want him to do is the only *right* thing for him. You cannot know, for only the Spirit *within* a man can know for himself. You have no right to interpose yourself between him and the God in his own soul; no right to steal silently into the inner portals of his being to turn him one way or the other. If you do so, remember the wrong you thus do another will invariably react upon yourself.

The only right you have to use the law of thought transference on another is to call out the Divine Self of him, saying to him silently something like this: "God lives in you; he guides all your actions; he leads you where he would have you go; he works in you to will and to do whatsoever he would have you to do," etc.; and then let the external manifestation be what it will, believing that it is just what God would have it for the present, even if it is exactly the opposite of what you had planned.

Another term often used, and not always clearly understood, is "chemicalization."

Did you ever put soda in sour milk, cider or other acid fluid and witness the agitation or excited action which takes place? One of the substances neutralizes the other, and something better results from the action.

This is a good illustration of what takes place sometimes in the minds and bodies of people. Suppose one has lived in wrong thought, and molded his body by wrong thought for years, until, as you might say, he has become solidified in that wrong belief. You introduce the truth to him by strong denials and affirmations as has been taught. The very newness of it (and because it is truth) creates the first few days new hope, new joy and health. After a little time a sort of mental ferment or agitation takes place. One is apt to feel very nervous and frightened away down in the depths of himself. If he has ever been sick, he will begin to feel the old diseases; if he has been morally bad, the old desires and habits will take possession of him with new force; if he has been holding denials and affirmations about business affairs until they have looked hopeful, all at once they collapse and seem darker and more hopeless than ever. All the new beliefs which lifted him into a new world for a few days seem failures, and he seems on the very verge of breaking up generally.

What has happened? Why, simply this: There has been a clash between the old condition—which was based on falsehood, fear and wrong ways of thinking—and the new thought or truth entering into him. The old mortal is kicking vigorously against the truth. He has a feeling of discouragement or fear—a feeling such as one would have

if caught at something disreputable. He should not
be frightened. That which he feels is, on the mental plane, a similar excitement and agitation to that
which was seen in the chemical action between the
alkali and acid on the material plane, *and something
higher and better always results.*

This agitation does not always take place with
every one, but is most apt to occur with those who
have been most fixed, and, as it were, solidified in
the old beliefs. Such people break up with more
resistance. Those who are not very settled in their
convictions are more malleable mentally and physically, and are not so apt to chemicalize. Vigorous
use of denials is also more apt to produce chemicalization than is the use of affimations. There is always less resistance by the mortal when it is gently
led into the truth than when its errors are directly
and vigorously combated. Should you find yourself
at any time in this state of internal excitement with
aggravation of old, bad conditions, it needs only that
you constantly affirm, "There is nothing to fear,
absolutely *nothing* to fear; perfect love reigns, and
all is good; peace, be still," etc., and very soon the
brighter conditions will appear and you will find
yourself on a much higher plane than you have ever
been before.

Do not be afraid of this word (or the condition) "chemicalization," as many have been, for truly there is nothing to fear in it.

The words "personality" and "individuality" are two words which present clearly distinct meanings to the trained mind, but to the untrained mind they are often used interchangeably and apart from their real meaning.

"Personality" applies to the mortal part of you —the mortal mind, the person, the external. It belongs to the region governed by the intellect. Your personality may be agreeable or disagreeable to others. When you say you dislike any one, you mean you dislike his personality—that exterior something which presents itself to us from the outside of any one. It is the outer, changeable man, in contradistinction to the inner or real man.

"Individuality" is the term used to denote the real man. The more God comes out into visibility through a person the more individualized he becomes. By this I do not mean that one's individuality is greater when he is more religious. Remember God is Wisdom, Intelligence, Love, Power, etc. The more pronounced manner in which any one of these qualities—or all of them—comes forth into visibility through a man, the greater his individuality.

Emerson was a man of large individuality, but small personality. He was grandly simple. He was of a shrinking, retiring nature (or personality). But just in proportion as the mortal of him was willing to retire and be thought little of, did the immortal, the God in him, shine forth in greater degree.

John the Baptist, who represents personality or the mortal, said in speaking of Jesus, who represents individuality or the divine, "He must increase, but I must decrease."

One's individuality is that part of him which never changes its identity. It is that which distinguishes one person from another. One's personality may become like that of others with whom he associates. Individuality never changes.

Do not confound the terms. One may have an aggressive, pronounced personality, or external man, which will, for a time, fight its way through obstacles and gain its point. But a pronounced individuality never battles; it is never puffed up; it is never governed by likes or dislikes or causes them in others; it is God come forth in greater degree through the soul of man, and all mere personality instinctively bends the knee before it in recognition of its superiority.

We cultivate individuality by listening to the

voice down deep within our own soul, and boldly following it, even if it does make us differ from others, as it surely will. We cultivate personality, in which lives pride, fear of criticism, and all manner of selfishness, by listening to the voices *outside* of ourselves, and being governed by selfish motives instead of by the highest within us. Seek always to cultivate, or bring into visibility, individuality, but never personality. In proportion as one increases, the other must decrease.

Whenever we fear any one, or shrink before him, it is because his personality, being the stronger, overcomes ours. Many timid souls go through life always feeling that they are inefficient, that others are wiser or better than they. They dread to meet a positive, self-conceited person; and when in the presence of such a one they are laid low, just as a field of tall wheat is after a fierce windstorm has swept across it. They feel as though they would like to get out of sight forever.

All this, dear timid ones, is not because your fellow really is wiser or better than you, but because his personality—the external, mortal man—is stronger than yours. You never have a similar feeling in the presence of strong individuality. Individuality in another not only produces in you an admiration for its superiority, but it also gives you, when in its presence, a strange new sense of your own inherent possibilities, which sense is full of exhilaration and comfort and encouragement to you. This is because a pronounced individuality simply means more of God come forth into visibility through the person, and by some mental process it has power to call forth more of God through you.

Now, if you want to know how to avoid being overcome and thrown off your feet by the strong personality of others, I will tell you:

Always remember that *personality is of the mortal, and individuality is of God.* Silently affirm your own individuality, your oneness with God, and your superiority to personality. Can God fear any person?

If you are naturally inclined to be timid or shrinking, make a practice of doing this until you overcome it: As you walk down the street and see any one coming toward you, even a stranger to you, silently affirm, "I am a part of God in visibility; I am one with the Father; this person has no power over me, for I am superior to all personality," etc. Cultivate this habit of thinking and affirming whenever you approach any person, and you will soon find that no personality, however strong and aggressive, has the power to throw you out of the most perfect self-poise. You will be self-possessed because God-possessed.

Some years ago I found myself under a sense of bondage to a strong, aggressive personality with whom, externally, I had been quite intimately associated for several months. I seemed to see things through another's eyes; and while I was more than half conscious of this, yet I could not seem to throw it off. This personality was able, with a very few words, to make me feel as though all I said or did was a mistake, and that I was a most miserable failure. I was always utterly discouraged after being in this presence, and felt that I had no ability to accomplish anything.

After vainly trying for weeks to free myself, one day I was walking along the street with a most intense desire and determination to be free. Many times before I had affirmed that this personality could not affect or overcome me, etc., but with no effect. This day I struck out further and declared (silently, of course), "There is no such personality in the universe as this one," affirming it again and again many times. After a few moments I began to feel wondrously lifted, and as though chains were dropping off. Then the voice within me urged me on a step further to say, "*There is no personality in the universe; there is nothing but God.*" After a short time spent in vigorously using these words, I seemed to break every fetter, and step out *absolutely free.* From that day to this, without further effort, I have been as free from any influence of that personality as though none had ever existed.

If at any time the lesser affirmation of truth fails to free you from the influence of other minds, try this more sweeping one—"There is no personality in the universe—there is nothing but God," and you are bound to be made free.

The more you learn to act from the voice within your own soul, the stronger and more pronounced will be individuality in you.

If inclined to wilt before strong personalities or mortal minds, always remember that, as Emerson puts it, "The soul [God] had need of such an organ as I." Since God has need of you, through which in some special manner to manifest himself—some manner which he cannot use any other organ for—what need have you to quail before any mere person, no matter how important he may feel himself to be?

However humble your place in life, however unknown to the world you may be, however small your capabilities may seem at present to you to be, you are just as much a *necessity* to God in his efforts to get himself into visibility as is the most brilliant intellect, the most thoroughly cultured person in the world. Remember this always, and act from the highest within *you*.

SPIRITUAL UNDERSTANDING OR REALIZATION

SEVENTH LESSON

Happy is the man that findeth wisdom, and the man that getteth understanding.

For the merchandise of it is better than the merchandise of silver, and the gain thereof than fine gold.

She is more precious than rubies: and all the things thou canst desire are not to be compared unto her.

Length of days is in her right hand; and in her left hand riches and honor.

Her ways are ways of pleasantness, and all her paths are peace.

She is a tree of life to them that lay hold upon her: and happy is every one that retaineth her.

With all thy getting, get understanding.

—Proverbs of Solomon.

What is this understanding upon the getting of which depends so much? Is it intellectual lore, gotten from delving deep into books of other men's making? Is it knowledge obtained from studying rocks (geology), or stars (astronomy), or even the human body (physiology)? Nay, verily, for when did such knowledge ever insure life and health and peace, ways of pleasantness, with riches and honor?

Understanding is a spiritual birth, a revelation

of God within the human soul. Jesus touched the root of the matter when, after having asked the disciples a certain question which was answered variously, according to the intellectual perception of the men, one—Peter—gave him a reply not based at all upon external reasoning, but upon intuition. He said to Peter, "Blessed art thou, Simon Barjona: for flesh and blood hath not revealed it unto thee, but my Father which is in heaven."

You may have an intellectual perception of the truth. You may easily grasp with the mind the statement that God is the Giver of all good gifts— life, health, love—just as people have for centuries grasped it. Or you may go further, and intellectually see that God is not only the Giver, but the Gift itself; that he *is* life, health, love, in us. But unless it be "revealed unto thee by my Father which is in heaven," it is of no practical benefit to you or to any one else.

This revelation of truth to the *consciousness* of a person is spiritual understanding.

You may say to yourself, or another may say silently to you, over and over again, that you are well and wise and happy. On the plane of mortal mind or intellect a certain "cure" is effected, and for a time you will feel well and wise and happy.

This is simply hypnotism, or mind cure. But until, down in the depths of your soul, you are *conscious* of your oneness with the Father, until you know within yourself that the spring of all wisdom and health and joy is within your own being, ready at any moment to spring forth at the call of your need, you have not understanding.

All the teachings of Jesus were for the purpose of leading men up to this consciousness of their oneness with the Father. He had to begin at the external man, because people then as now were living mostly in external things, and teach him to love his enemies, to do good to others, etc. These were external steps for them to take—a sort of lopping off the ends of the branches; but they were steps which led on up to the place of desire and attainment where finally the Master could tell them some of the "many things" which previously they "could not bear."

He told them of the Comforter which should be *in* them, and which should teach them all things, revealing the "deep things of God" to them, and showing them things to come. In other words, he told these simple, worldly-ignorant men how they might find the kingdom of heaven *within* themselves—the kingdom of love, of power, of life.

The coming of the Comforter to their hearts and lives, giving them power over every form of sin, sickness, sorrow, and even death itself, is exactly what we mean by understanding or realization. The power which this consciousness of the indwelling Father gives is as much for us today as it was for them to whom the Nazarene verbally spoke. Aye, more; for did he not say, "Greater works than these shall ye do"?

All the foregoing lessons have been just simply external stepping-stones leading up to this same point—the consciousness of the ever-abiding inner Presence, which is to reveal to each soul the fact that it (the soul) is the temple in which dwells the Most High God. "Know ye not that your body is the temple of the Holy Ghost which is in you?"

I cannot reveal God to you. You cannot reveal God to another. If I have learned, I may tell you, and you may tell another how to seek and find God, each within his own soul. But the new birth into the consciousness of our spiritual faculties and possibilities is indeed like the wind which "bloweth where it listeth, and thou hearest the sound thereof, but canst not tell whence it cometh, and whither it goeth: so is every one that is born of the Spirit." It is a process in the silence, in the invisible.

Intellectual lore can be bought and sold; understanding or realization cannot. A man, Simon by name, once attempted to buy the power which spiritual understanding gives, from another who possessed it. "But Peter said unto him, Thy money perish with thee, because thou hast thought that the gift of God may be purchased with money. Thou hast neither part nor lot in this matter: for thy heart is not right in the sight of God."

Neither will crying and beseeching bring spiritual understanding. Hundreds of people have tried this method, and have not received that for which they earnestly but ignorantly sought. They have not received, because *they did not know how to take* that which God freely offered. Others have sought this spiritual understanding or consciousness of the indwelling Father with selfish motives, because of the power it would give them. "Ye ask, and receive not, because ye ask amiss, that ye may consume it upon your lusts" (or to serve selfish ends).

Understanding, or realization of the presence of God within us, is as Peter said, "the gift of God." It comes to any and all who learn how to seek it aright. Emerson says, "This energy [or consciousness of God in the soul] does not descend into individual life on any other condition than entire possession. It comes to the lowly and simple; it comes to whomsoever will put off what is foreign and proud; it comes as insight; it comes as serenity and grandeur. When we see those whom it inhabits, we are apprised of new degrees of greatness. From that inspiration [or consciousness] the man comes back with a changed tone. He does not talk with men with an eye to their opinion; he . . . is plain ˎ and true; has no rose color, no fine friends, . . . no adventures; does not want admiration; dwells in the hour that now is."

"And ye shall seek me, and find me, when ye shall search for me with all your heart." In that day when, more than riches and honor and power and selfish glory, you shall desire spiritual understanding, in that day will come to you the revelation of God in your own soul, and you will be conscious of the indwelling Father, who is life and strength and power and peace.

One may so desire a partial revelation of God within him, a revelation along one line—as, for instance, that of health—as to seek it with "all his heart." And if he has learned how to *take* the desired gift, by uncompromising affirmation that it is his already, he will get understanding or realization of God as his perfect health. So with any other de-

sired gift of God. This is a step in the right direction. It is learning how to *take God by faith* for
whatever one desires. But in the onward growth
the time will come to every soul when he will hear
the Divine Voice within him saying, "Come up
higher," and he will pass beyond any merely selfish
desires which are just for his own comfort's sake.
He will desire good that he may have the more to
give out, knowing that as God (or Good) flows
through him to others it will make him "every whit
whole."

In the beginning of Solomon's reign as king over
Israel, the Divine Presence apeared to him in a
dream at night, saying, "Ask what I shall give thee."
And Solomon said, "Give thy servant an understanding heart."

"And the speech pleased the Lord, that Solomon had asked this thing.

"And God said unto him, Because thou hast
asked this thing, and hast not asked for thyself long
life; neither hast asked riches for thyself, nor hast
asked the life of thine enemies; but hast asked for
thyself understanding to discern judgment;

"Behold, I have done according to thy words:
lo, I have given thee a wise and an understanding
heart; so that there was none like thee before thee,

neither after thee shall any rise like unto thee.

"And I have also given thee that which thou hast not asked, both riches and honor: so that there shall not be any among the kings like unto thee all thy days."

Thus in losing sight of all worldly goods and chattles, all merely selfish ends, and desiring above all things an understanding heart (or a spiritual consciousness of God within him as wisdom, life, power), Solomon received all the goods or good things included, so that there was none among the kings like unto him in worldly possessions. "Seek ye *first* the kingdom [or consciousness] of God, and his righteousness; and all these things shall be added unto you." "For whosoever will save his life [or the things of his life] shall lose it: and whosoever will lose his life for my sake [or that is willing to forget the goods of this life for the truth's sake, choosing before all things the finding of God in his own soul] shall find it."

When you first consciously desire spiritual understanding you do not attain it at once. You have been living in the external of your being, and have believed yourself cut off from God. Your first step after "coming to yourself" is to "arise and go to my Father"—to turn your thoughts away from the ex-

ternal seeming toward the central and real; to know
intellectually that you are not cut off from God, and
that he forever desires to manifest himself within you
as your present deliverance from all suffering and
sin.   Just as Jesus taught, we begin our journey toward understanding by cutting off the branches of
our selfishness.   We try to love instead of hating.
We begin to forgive, even if it costs us great mental
effort, instead of avenging ourselves.   We begin to
deny envy, jealousy, anger, sickness, and all imper-
fection, and to affirm love, peace and health.

Begin with the words of truth which you have
learned, and which perhaps you have as yet only
comprehended with the intellect.   You must be willing to thus take the very first light you receive and
use it faithfully, earnestly, both to help yourself and
others.   Sometimes you will be almost overcome by
questions and doubts arising in your own mind when
looking in vain for results.   But you must with effort press past the place of doubt; and some day,
in the fullness of God's time, while you are using
the words of truth, they will suddenly be illumined
and become to you the living word within you—the
true light which lighteth every man that cometh into
the world.   You will no longer dwell in darkness,
for the light will be within your own soul; and the

"word will be made flesh" to you; *i. e.*, you will
be conscious of a new and diviner life in your body,
a new and diviner love for all people, a new and
diviner power to accomplish.

This is spiritual understanding. This is a flash
of the Most High God within your consciousness.
Old things will have passed away. Behold, all
things become new! This will be the time when
you "will not talk with men with an eye to their
opinion." This is when you will suddenly become
plain and true; when you will cease to desire admiration; when all words of congratulation from
others on your success will fill you with an inex-
pressible sense of humility; when all mere compli-
ments will be to you as sounding brass and tinkling
cymbal. Truly, from that inspiration a man comes
back with a changed tone!

With spiritual understanding comes new light on
the Scriptures. The very Spirit of Truth, which
has come to abide with you forever in your consciousness, takes of the deep things of God and reveals them unto you. You no longer feel like running to and fro to teachers or healers, however ef-
ficient and good they may be. You know that the
living light, the living word within you, will guide
you into all truth.

What we need to do is to seek this revelation of the living Christ within our own being, each for himself, knowing that only this divinity come forth can make us grand and powerful and happy.

Every person in his heart desires, though he may not yet quite know it, this new birth into a higher life, into this spiritual consciousness. Everyone wants more power, more good, more joy. And though to the ignorant mind it may seem that it is more money as money, or more goods that he wants, it is, nevertheless, more of good (or God) that he craves; for all good is God.

Many today are conscious that the inner hunger cannot be satisfied with goods, and are with all earnestness seeking this spiritual understanding or consciousness of an immanent God; they have been seeking long, and with a great degree of unselfishness, a feeling that when they have fully found God they will begin to do for others. Faithful service for others hastens the day-dawning for ourselves. The gifts of God are not given in reward for faithful service, as a fond mother gives cake to her child for being good; nevertheless they are a reward, inasmuch as that service is one of the steps which lead up to the place where all the fullness of God awaits us. And while spiritual understanding is in reality a "gift of God," it comes to us more or less quickly in proportion as we use the light we already have in helping others.

I believe that too much introspection, too much of what people usually call "spiritual seeking," is detrimental rather than helpful to the end desired—spiritual growth. It is a sort of spiritual selfishness, paradoxical as this may seem. From the beginning to the end Jesus taught the giving out of what one already possessed to him who had none.

"Is not this the fast that I have chosen?" said the Spirit of God through the prophet Isaiah, "to loose the bands of wickedness, to undo the heavy burdens, and to let the oppressed go free?

"Is it not to deal thy bread to the hungry, and that thou bring the poor that are cast out to thy house? when thou seest the naked, that thou cover him?

"Then shall thy light break forth as the morning, and thine health shall spring forth speedily. Then shalt thou call, and the Lord shall answer, Here I am.

"And if thou draw out thy soul to the hungry, and satisfy the afflicted soul; then shall thy light rise in obscurity, and thy darkness be as the noonday:

"And the Lord shall guide thee continually, and

satisfy thy soul in drouth, and make fat thy bones:
and thou shalt be like a watered garden, and like a
spring of water, whose waters fail not."

Stagnation is death. A pool cannot be kept
clean and sweet and renewed unless there is an outlet as well as an inlet. It is our business to keep the
outlet open, and God's business to keep the stream
flowing in and through us. Unless you use for the
service of others what God has already given you,
you will find it a long, weary road to spiritual understanding.

We cry out and strain every nerve to obtain full
understanding, just as sometimes we have heard earnest people, but people wholly ignorant of divine
laws, beseech God for the "full baptism of the Holy
Ghost as in the day of Pentecost." Jesus said, "I
have yet many things to say unto you, but ye cannot
bear them now." We grow by using for others the
light and knowledge we have. We expand, as we
go on step by step in spiritual insight, until in the
fullness of time, which means when we have grown
spiritually up to the place where God sees we are
able to bear the many things, we receive the desire of
our hearts—understanding.

Seek your own Lord. Take the light as it is revealed to you and use it for others; and prove for

yourself whether there be truth in this prophecy of Isaiah, that "then shall thy light rise in obscurity, and thy darkness be as the noonday;" and "then shall thy light break forth as the morning, and thine health shall spring forth speedily."

THE SECRET PLACE OF THE MOST HIGH

EIGHTH LESSON

[In the progress of these simple lessons, some may object to the language being too "orthodox"—too much of the religious side of the question. I use Scriptural terms simply because I prefer them; but it is all essentially one and the same thing. It is not Mental Science nor Christian Science, as such, that you want. It is not any *ism*, for each is but one side of the truth. It is *truth* we are after; and at the center of all these various forms of presenting the truth the thing itself is one.

So let us be big enough and broad enough, no matter on what side of the truth we have thus far been seeking the light of the world, to put away all prejudices, all the limitations which the mere form of words may heretofore have made in our minds, and be open to all there is for us.]

There is nothing the human soul so longs for, so cries out after, as to know God, "whom to know aright is life eternal."

With a restlessness which is pitiful to see, people are ever shifting from one thing to another, always hoping to find rest and satisfaction in some anticipated accomplishment or possession. Men fancy they want houses and lands, great learning or power. They pursue these things and gain them only to find themselves still restless, still unsatisfied.

At the great heart of humanity there is a deep and awful homesickness, which never has been and never can be satisfied with anything less than a clear, vivid consciousness of the *indwelling* presence of God, our Father. In all ages earnest men and women, who have recognized this inner hunger as the heart's cry after God, have left seeking after *things*, and have sought, by devoted worship and by service to others, to enter into this consciousness; but few have succeeded in reaching the promised place where their "joy is full." Others have hoped and feared alternately; they have tried with the best knowledge they possessed to "work out their salvation," not yet having learned that there must be an *in*-working as well as an *out*-working. "By grace [or free gift] ye are saved through *faith;* and that not of yourselves [or of any mortal working] : *it is the gift of God:* Not of works, lest any man should boast."

To him who "dwelleth in the secret place of the Most High" there is promised immunity from the noisome pestilence and the snare of the fowler, from the terror by night, and the arrow that flieth by day; and even immunity from *fear* of these things. Oh, the awfully paralyzing effect of fear of evil! It surely "doth make cowards of us all." It makes us helpless as babes. It makes us pigmies, where we might be giants were we only free from it. It is at the root of all our failures, nearly all sickness, poverty and distress. But we have the promise of deliverance from even the fear of evil when we are in the "secret place." "Thou shalt not be afraid of the terror by night," etc. "In the time of trouble he shall hide me in his pavilion: in the secret of his tabernacle shall he hide me." "Thou shalt hide them in the secret of thy presence from the pride of man: thou shalt keep them secretly in a pavilion from the strife of tongues."

The secret place! Why called a *secret* place? What is it? Where may we find it? how abide in it?

It is a secret place because it is the place of meeting between the Christ at the center of your being and your consciousness—a hidden place into which no outside person can either induct you or enter himself. We must drop the idea that this place of realization of our divinity can be given to us by any human being. No one can come into it from the outside. Hundreds of earnest souls are seeking night and day to get this inner revealing. They run from teacher to teacher, many of them making the most frantic efforts to meet the financial obligations thus incurred.

You may study with human teachers and from man-made books till doomsday; you may get all the theological lore of the ages; you may understand intellectually all the statements of truth, and be able to prate healing formulæ as glibly as oil flows; but until there is a definite *inner revealing* of the reality of an indwelling Christ through whom and by whom cometh life, health, peace, power, *all* things—aye, who *is* all things—you have not yet found the "secret of the Lord."

In order to gain this knowledge—this consciousness of God within their own soul—many are willing (and wisely so, for this is greater than all other knowledge) to spend all they possess. Even Paul, after twenty-five years of service and of most marvelous preaching, said, "I count all things but loss for the excellency of the knowledge of Christ Jesus my Lord: and do count them but dung, that I may win Christ" (or the consciousness of his Divine Self).

Beloved, that which you so earnestly desire and seek will never be found by seeking it through the mental side alone, any more than it has heretofore been found through the emotional side alone. Intuition and intellect are meant to travel together, in-

tuition always holding the reins to guide intellect.
"Come, and let us *reason together*, saith the Lord."
If you have been thus far on the way cultivating and
enlarging only the mental side of truth, as probably
is the case, you need, in order to come into the fullness of understanding, to let the mental, the reasoning, side rest awhile. "Become as a little child,"
and, learning how to be still, *listen* to that which the
Father will say to you through the intuitional part of
your being. The light you so crave *will* come out of
the deep silence, and become manifest to you from
within you, if you will but keep still and look for it
from that source.

This conscious knowledge of an indwelling God
which we so crave is that of which Paul wrote to the
Colossians, as "the mystery which hath been hid
from ages and from generations, but now is made
manifest . . . *Christ in you*, the hope of glory."
"The secret place of the Most High," where each
one of us may dwell and be safe from all harm or
fear of evil, is the point of mystical union between
soul (or conscious mind) and Spirit (or God in us),
wherein we no longer believe, but we *know*, that
God in Christ abides always at the center of our
being as our perfect health, deliverance, prosperity,
power, ready to come forth at any moment we claim

it into manifestation. We know it. We *know* it. We feel our oneness with the Father, and we manifest this oneness.

To possess the secret of anything gives one the power over it. This personal, conscious knowledge of the Father in us is the secret which is the key to all power. What we want is the revelation to us of this marvelous "secret." What shall, who can give it to us except He, the "Spirit of Truth, which proceedeth from the Father"? Surely none other. That which God would say to you, and do through you, is a great secret which no man on the face of the earth knows, or ever will know, except yourself as it is revealed to you by the Spirit which is *in you*. That secret which He tells me, is not revealed to you, nor yours to me; but each soul must, after all is said and done, deal directly with the Father *through the Son within himself.*

Secrets are not told upon the housetop. Nor is it possible to pass this, the greatest of secrets, from one to another. God, the Creator of our being, must himself whisper it to each soul living in the very innermost of itself. "To him that overcometh [or is consciously in process of overcoming] will I give to eat of the *hidden* manna, and will give him a white stone [or a mind like a clean white tablet], and in the stone *a new name written, which no man knoweth saving he that receiveth it.*" It is so secret that it cannot even be put into human language or repeated by human lips.

What you want today, and what I want, is that the *words* which we have learned to say as truth be made alive to us. We want a revelation of God in us as Life, to be made to our own personal consciousness as health. We no longer care to have somebody just tell us the words from the outside. We want a revelation of God as Love within us, so that our whole being is filled and thrilled with love—a love that does not have to be pumped up by a determined effort because we know that it is right to love and wrong not to love, but a love that flows with the spontaneity and fullness of an artesian well, because it is so full at the bottom that it *must* flow out or burst.

What we want today is a revelation to our consciousness of God within us as Omnipotent Power, so that we can by a word or look "accomplish that whereunto the word is sent." We want the manifestation *to us of* the Father *in us,* so that we can know him personally. We want to be conscious of "God working in us to will and to do," so that we may "work out our salvation." We have been learning how to do the *out*-working, but have now come up to a point when we must learn more of how to place ourselves in an attitude where we can each one be conscious of the Divine *inner* working.

Mary talked with the risen Jesus, supposing it was the gardener, until suddenly, as he spoke her name, there flashed into her consciousness a ray of pure intelligence, and in an instant the revelation was made to her innermost soul of his identity.

According to the same sacred history, Thomas Didymus had walked daily for three years with the most wondrous teacher of spiritual things that has ever lived. He had watched this teacher's life and been partaker of his very presence, physical and mental. He had had just what you and I have thus far received of mental training and external teaching. But there came a time when there was an inner revealing which made him exclaim, "*My* Lord and *my* God!" The secret name which no other man could know for him had that moment been given to him. There had come, in the twinkling of an eye, the manifestation to his consciousness of the Father in him as *his* Lord and *his* God. No longer simply our Father and our Lord, but *my* Lord and *my* God—my Divine Self revealed to me personally.

Is not this that which you are craving?

Each soul must come to a time when it no longer is satisfied with or seeks external helps—when it knows that the inner revelation of "*my* Lord and *my* God" to its consciousness can only come to it through an Indwelling Power, which has been there all the time, waiting with an infinite longing, but an infinite patience, to reveal the Father to the child.

This revelation will never come through the intellect of man to the consciousness, but must ever come *through* the intuitional to the intellect as a manifestation of Spirit to the soul. "The natural man receiveth not [nor can it impart them] the things of the Spirit of God: for they are foolishness unto him: neither can he know them, because they are spiritually discerned," and they must be spiritually imparted.

In our eagerness we have waited upon every source we could reach or hear for the light we wanted. Because we have not known how to wait upon the Spirit within us for the desired revelation, we have run to and fro. Let no one misunderstand me in what I say about withdrawing yourself from teachers. Teachers are good and are necessary up to a certain point. "How then shall they call on him in whom they have not believed? and how shall they believe in him of whom they have not heard? and how shall they hear without a preacher?"

Books and lectures are good, teachers are good,
until you learn by the hearing of the ear that Christ,
the Son of God, lives *in* you; that he within you is
your light and life and all. When you have once
grasped this beyond a doubt with the intellect, you
are forever through with external teachers; and
every day you look to them after this you put off the
day of revelation for yourself. That Christ *lives* in
you, Spirit itself must make real to you. Teachers
talk about the light, but the light itself must flash into
the darkness before you can see the light.

Had the Master remained with the disciples, I
doubt if they would ever have gotten beyond the
place of hanging on his words and following in the
footsteps of his personality. With the knowledge
and power he possessed he might at any time have
spoken the word which would have opened the eyes
of their understanding; but he did not.

Jesus knew that his treatments for spiritual illumination, given to his disciples from his recognition of
truth, would act in them as a seed thought, but he
also knew that each man must *for himself* wait upon
God for the inner illumination which should be last-
ing and real. God alone could whisper the secret
to each one separately.

The "enduement of power" was not to come to

them by the spoken word through another personality, even that of Jesus with his great spiritual power and discernment. It was to come from "on high" to each individual consciousness. It was the "promise of the Father which ye have heard of me." He had merely told them about it, but had no power to give it to them.

So to each of us this spiritual illumination which we are crying out after, this "enduement of power" for which we are willing to sell all that we have, must come from "on high," *i. e.*, to the consciousness from the Spirit within our being. This is the secret which the Father longs with an infinite yearning to reveal to each individual soul. It is because of the Father's desire within us to show us the secret, that we are drawn to desire the revelation. It is the purpose for which we came into the world—that we might grow step by step, as we are doing, to the place where we could bear to have the secret of his inner abiding revealed to us.

Do not be confused by seeming contradictions in the lessons. I have said heretofore that too much introspection is not good. I repeat it; for there are those who, in earnest desire to know God, are always seeking the light for themselves, but neglect to use that which they already have to help others.

There must be an equal conscious receiving from the Father and giving out to the world, a perfect equilibrium between the inflowing and the outgiving, to keep perfect harmony. We must each learn how to wait renewedly upon God for the infilling, and then go and give out that which we have received to every creature, as the Spirit leads us to give, either in preaching or teaching, or in silently living the truth. That which *fills* us will radiate from us without effort right in the place in life where we stand.

In nearly all teaching of truth from the purely mental side there is much said about the working out of our salvation by holding right thoughts, by denials and affirmations. This is all good. But there is also another side which we need to know a little more about. We must learn how to be still and let Spirit, the "I Am," work in us, that we may indeed be made "new creatures," that we may have the mind of Christ in all things.

When you have learned how to perfectly abandon yourself to Infinite Spirit, and have seasons of doing this daily, you will be surprised at the marvelous change which will be wrought in you without any conscious effort of your own.

It will search far below your conscious mind, and root out things in your nature of which you have scarcely been conscious, simply because they have lain latent there, waiting for something to bring them out. It will work into your consciousness light and life and love and all good, perfectly filling all your lack while you just quietly *wait and receive*. Of the practical steps in this direction we will speak in another lesson.

Paul, who had learned this way of faith, this way of being still, and letting the "I Am" work itself into his conscious mind as the fullness of all his needs, was neither afraid nor ashamed to say:

"For this cause I bow my knees unto the Father of our Lord Jesus Christ,

"Of whom the whole family in heaven and earth is named,

"That he would grant you, according to the riches of his glory, to be strengthened with might by his Spirit in the inner man;

"That Christ may dwell in your hearts by faith; that ye, being rooted and grounded in love,

"May be able to comprehend with all saints what is the breadth, and length, and depth, and height;

"And to know the love of Christ, *which passeth knowledge*, that ye might be filled with all the fullness of God."

And then he gives an ascription of praise: "Unto him that is able to do exceedingly abundantly above all that we ask or think, *according to the power that worketh in us.*"

FINDING THE SECRET PLACE

NINTH LESSON

How to seek? Where to find? How to abide in it? These are the questions that today more than at any other time in the history of the world are engaging the hearts of men. More than anything else it is what I want. It is what you want.

All these steps we are taking, by speaking the words of truth and striving to manifest the light we have already received, are carrying us on swiftly to the time when we shall have consciously the perfect mind of Christ, with all the love and beauty and health and power which that implies.

We need not be anxious or in a hurry for the full manifestation. Let us not at any time lose sight of the fact that our desire, great as it is, is only God's desire in us. "No man cometh unto me, except the Father draw him." The Father in us desires to reveal the secret of his presence to us, else we had not known any hunger for the secret, or for truth.

"Ye have not chosen me, but I have chosen you, and ordained you, that ye should go and bring forth fruit."

108

Whoever you are that read these words, where-
ever you stand in the world, be it on the platform
preaching the gospel, or in the humblest little home
seeking the truth that you may make it manifest in
a sweeter, stronger, less selfish life, know once and
forever it is not you seeking God, but it is God seeking you. That which you feel and desire for greater
manifestation is the Eternal Energy, which holds
the worlds in their orbits, *out-pushing* through you
to get into fuller manifestation. You need not
worry. You need not be anxious. You need not
strive. Only *let* it. Learn how to *let* it.

After all our beating about the bush, seeking
here and there for our heart's desire, we must come
right to him who himself is the fulfillment of every
desire; who waits to manifest more of himself to us
and through us. If you wanted my love or anything that I *am* (not that I *have*), you would not go
to Tom Jones or Mary Smith to get it. Either of
these persons might tell you I could and would give
myself, but you would have to come directly to me,
and receive of me that which only I have, because
I *am* it.

And in some way, after all our seeking for the
light and truth, we must learn *how to wait, each one*

for himself, upon God for this inner revelation of truth, and our oneness with him.

The light we want is not some *thing* God has to give. It is God himself. God does not give us life or love as a thing. God is Life and Light and Love. More of himself in our consciousness, then, is what we all want, no matter what other name we may give it.

My enduement of power must come from "on high," from a higher region within myself than my present conscious mind; so must yours. It must be a descent of the Holy (whole, entire, complete) Spirit at the center of your being into your conscious mind. The illumination we want can never come in any other way; nor can the power to make good manifest.

We hear a great deal about "sitting in the silence." To many it does not mean very much, for they have not yet learned how to "wait upon God," or to hear any voice except external ones. Noise belongs to the outside world, not to God. God works in the stillness, and we can so wait upon the Father of our being as to be conscious of the still, inner working—conscious of the fulfillment of our desires. "They that seek the Lord shall not want any good." "They that wait upon the Lord shall renew their strength."

In one of Edward Everett Hale's stories he speaks of a little girl who, amidst her play with the butterflies and birds in a country place, used to run into a nearby chapel frequently to pray; and after praying would always remain perfectly still a few minutes, "waiting," she said, "to see if God wanted to say anything" to her. So children are always nearest the kingdom.

When beginning the practice of sitting in the silence, do not feel that you must go and sit with some other person. The presence of another personality is apt to distract the mind. Learn first how to commune alone with the Creator of the universe, who is all companionship. And when you are able to withdraw from the outside, and be alone with him, then sitting with others may be profitable to you and to them.

"Sitting in the silence" is not just a sort of lazy drifting. It is a passive, but a definite, *waiting upon God.* When you want to do this, take a time when you are not likely to be disturbed, and when you can for a little while lay off all care. Begin your silence by lifting up your heart in prayer to the Father of your being. Do not be afraid that if you

begin to pray you will be too "orthodox." You are
not going to *supplicate* a God who has already given
you "all things whatsoever ye desire." You have
already learned that before you call he has sent that
which you desire; otherwise you would not desire it.

You know better than to plead to or beseech
God with an unbelieving prayer. But spending the
first few moments of your silence to the outside
world, in speaking directly to the Father, centers
your mind on the Eternal. Many who earnestly try
to get still and wait upon God have found that the
moment they sit down and close their eyes, the
thoughts, instead of being concentrated, are filled
with every sort of vain imagination. The most
trivial things, from the fixing of a shoe-string to the
gossipy conversation of a week ago, will chase each
other in rapid succession through the mind, and at
the end of an hour they have gained nothing. This
is to them discouraging.

This is but a natural result of trying not to think
at all. Nature abhors a vacuum, and if you make
(or try to) your mind a vacuum, the thought images
of others which fill the atmosphere about you will
rush in to fill it, leaving you as far away from the
consciousness of the Divine Presence as ever. You

can prevent this by beginning your silence with prayer.

It is always easier for the mind to say realizingly, "Thy will is being done in me now," after having prayed, "Let thy will be done in me." It is always easier to say with realization, "God flows through me as life and peace and power," after having prayed, "Let thy life flow through me anew while I wait." Of course it does not change God's attitude towards us, but it is easier for the human mind to take several successive steps with firmness and assurance than for it to take one big, bold leap to a point of eminence and hold itself steady there. While you are thus concentrating your thoughts upon God, in definite conversation with the Author of your being, no outside thought images can possibly rush in to torment or distract you. Your mind, instead of being open and negative towards the external, is closed to it, and open only to God, the Source of all the good you desire.

Of course there is to be no set form of words used. But sometimes using words like, for instance, the first few verses of the 103d Psalm, in the beginning of the silent communion, makes it a matter of face-to-face speaking: "Thou forgivest all my iniquities [or mistakes] ; thou healest all my diseases;

thou redeemest my life from destruction, and crown-
est me with lovingkindness, now, *now*, while I wait
upon thee;" sometimes entering into the innermost
with the words of a familiar hymn, as

"Thou art the Life within me,
O Christ, thou King of kings;
Thou art thyself the answer
To all my questionings."

Repeat the words over many times, not anxiously
nor with strained effort, not reaching out and up
and away off to an outside God; but let it be the
quiet, earnest uplifting of the heart to a higher something right within itself, even to the "Father in me."
Let it be with the quietness and assurance of a child
speaking to its loving father.

Too many people carry in their faces a strained,
white look that comes from an abnormal "sitting in
the silence," as they term it. It is hard for them to
know that God is right here within them, and when
sitting they fall into the way of reaching away out
and up after him. Such are earnest souls truly feeling after God if haply they may find him, when all
the time he is near them, even in their very hearts.
Do not reach out thus. This is as though a seed
were planted in the earth, and just because it recognized a vivifying, life-giving principle in the sun's

rays, it began to strain and stretch itself upward and outward to get more of the sun. You can see at a glance that by so doing it would get no solid root whatever in the earth where God intended it to be. All the plant needs to do is to keep its face turned toward the sun, and *let itself be drawn upward* by the sun.

Some of us, in our desire to grow, and having recognized the necessity of waiting upon God in the stillness for the vivifying and renewal of life, make the mistake of climbing up and away from our body. Such abnormal outstretching and upreaching is neither wise nor profitable. After a little of it one begins to get cold feet and congested head. While the soul is thus reaching out the body is left alone, and it becomes correspondingly weak and negative. This is all wrong. We are not to reach out away from the body even after the Sun of Righteousness. We are rather to be still, and *let the Sun shine on us right where we are.* Why, the sun *draws* the seed up as fast as it can bear it and be strong. We have not got to grow ourselves, only to *let* the Sun grow us.

But we are to *consciously let* it; not merely to take the attitude of negatively letting it by not opposing it, but put ourselves consciously where the

Sun can shine upon us, and then "be still and *know*" that while we wait there it is doing the work. While waiting upon God we should, as much as possible, relax ourselves both mentally and physically. To use a very homely but practical illustration, take much such an attitude of the entire being as do the fowls when taking a sun-bath in the sand. And yet there is something more than a *dead passivity* to be maintained through it all. There must be a sort of conscious active *taking* of that which God gives freely to the waiting soul.

Let me see if I can make it plain. We first withdraw ourselves bodily and mentally from the outside world. We "enter into thy closet and shut the door" (the closet of our being, the very innermost of ourselves), by turning our thoughts within. Just say, "Thou abidest within me; thou art alive there now; thou hast all power; thou art *now* the answer to all I desire; thou dost now radiate thyself from the center of my being to the circumference, and out into the visible world as the fullness of my desires." Then be still, absolutely still. Relax every part of your being, and believe that it is being done. The Divine Substance does flow in at the center and out into the visible world every moment you wait; for it is an immutable law that "he that asketh receiveth," and it will come forth as the "fulfillment of your desire" if you *expect* it to. "According to your faith be it unto you."

If you find your mind wandering, bring it right back by saying again, "It is being done; thou art working in me; I am receiving that which I desire," etc. Do not look for signs and wonders, but just be still and *know* that the very thing you want is flowing in, and will come forth into manifestation either at once or a little further on.

Go even beyond this and speak words of thanksgiving to this innermost Presence, that it has heard and answered, that it does now come forth into visibility. There is something about the mental act of thanksgiving that seems to carry the human mind far beyond the region of doubt into the clear atmosphere of faith and trust, where "all things are possible." Even if at first you are not conscious of having received anything from God, do not worry or cease from your thanksgiving. Do not go back of it again to the asking, but continue giving thanks that while you waited you did receive, and that it is now manifest; and believe me, you will soon rejoice and give thanks, not rigidly from sense of duty, but because of the sure manifest fulfillment of your desire.

Do not let waiting in silence become a bondage to you. If you find yourself getting into a strained attitude of mind, or "heady," get up and go about some external work for a time. Or, if you find your mind will wander, do not insist; for the moment you get into a rigid mental attitude you shut off all inflow of the Divine into your consciousness. There must be a sort of relaxed passivity, and yet an active taking it by faith. Shall I call it an active passivity?

Of course, as we go on in spiritual understanding and desire, we very soon come to the place where we want more than anything else that the desires of Infinite Wisdom and Love be fulfilled in us. "My thoughts are not your thoughts, neither are your ways my ways, saith the Lord. For as the heavens are higher than the earth, so are my ways higher than your ways, and my thoughts than your thoughts."

Our desires are God's desires, but in a *limited degree*. And we soon throw aside our limitations, our circumscribed desires (as soon, at least, as we see that more of God means more of good and joy and happiness), and with all our souls cry out in the silent sitting, "Fulfill *thy highest* thought in me now!" We make ourselves as clay in the potter's hands, willing to be molded anew, to be "changed into the same image," to be made after the mind of the indwelling Christ.

We repeat from time to time, while waiting, words something like these: "Thou art now renewing me according to thy highest thought for me; thou art radiating thy very Self throughout my entire being, making me like unto thyself, for there is nothing else but thee. Father, I thank thee, I thank thee." Be still, be still while he works. "Not by might, nor by power, but by my Spirit, saith the Lord of hosts."

While you thus wait, and let him, he will work marvelous changes in you. You will have a strange, new consciousness of serenity and quiet, a feeling that something has been done, that some new power to overcome has come unto you. You will be able to say, "I and the Father are one," with a new meaning, a new sense of reality and awe that will make you feel very still. Oh, how one conscious touch of the Oversoul makes all life seem different! All the hard things become easy; the troublesome things no longer have power to worry; the rasping people and things of the world lose all their aforetime power to annoy. Why? Because, for the time, we see things from the Christ side of ourselves; we see as he sees. We do not have to deny evil;

we *know* in that moment that it is nothing at all. We no longer rigidly affirm the good from sense of duty, but with delight and spontaneity, because we cannot help it. It is *revealed* to us as good. Faith has become reality.

Do not be discouraged if you do not at once get conscious results in this silent sitting. Every moment that you wait the Spirit *is* working to make you a new creature in Christ—a creature possessing consciously his very own qualities and powers. There may be a working for days before you see any change; but it will surely come. And you will soon get so you can go into the silence, into conscious communion with your Lord, at a moment's notice, at any time, in any place.

There is no conflict or inconsistency between this waiting upon God to be made perfect, and the way of "speaking the word" out toward the external to make perfection visible. Waiting upon and consciously receiving from the Source only makes the outspeaking (the holding of right thoughts and words) easy, instead of laborious. Try it and see.

Clear revelation—the word made *alive* as truth to our consciousness—*must* come to every soul who continues to wait upon God. But remember, there are two conditions imposed. You are to *wait* upon

God, not simply to run in and out, but to abide, to *dwell* in the secret place of the Most High.

Of course I do not mean that you are to give *all* the time to sitting alone in meditation and silence, but that your mind shall be continually in an attitude of waiting upon God, an attitude not of clamoring for *things*, but of listening for the Father's voice and expecting a manifestation of the Father to your consciousness.

Jesus, our Master in spiritual knowledge and power, had many hours of lone communion with his Father, and his greatest works were done after these. So may we, so *must* we, commune alone with the Father if we would manifest the Christ. But Jesus did not spend all his time in *receiving*. He poured forth into everyday use, among the children of men in the ordinary vocations of life, that which he received of his Father. His knowledge of spiritual things was used constantly to uplift and help other people. We must do likewise; for newness of life and revelation flows in the faster as we give out that which we have to help others. "Go teach and preach and heal," he said. Go *manifest* the Christ within you, which ye have received of the Father. God works *in* us to will and to do, but we must work *out* our salvation.

The second indispensable condition of finding
the secret place and abiding in it is "my expectation
is from Him"—"My soul, wait thou only upon
God; for my expectation is from him." "Truly in
vain is salvation hoped for from the hills, and from
the multitude of mountains: truly in the Lord our
God is the salvation of Israel." "It is good that a
man should both hope and quietly wait for the salvation of the Lord."

Is your expectation from him, or is it from books,
or teachers, or friends, or meetings, or societies?

"The King of Israel, even the Lord, is in the
midst of *thee*." Think of it! *In the midst of thee*
—at the center of thy being this moment while you
read these words. Say it, say it, think it, dwell
upon it, whoever you are, wherever you are! In the
midst of *thee!* Then what need for all this running
around? What need for all this strained outreach-
ing after him?

"The Lord thy God in the midst of thee is
mighty [not God in the midst of another, but in the
midst of thee, *thyself*, standing right where you are] ;
he will save, he will rejoice over thee with joy; he
will rest in his love, he will joy over thee with singing." You are his love. It is you he will rejoice in
with singing if you will turn away from people to

him within you. And his singing and joy will so fill you that your life will be a great thanksgiving.

Your Lord is not my Lord, nor my Lord your Lord. Your Lord is the Christ within your own being. My Lord is the Christ within my soul.

One Spirit, one Father of all, in us all, but different manifestations or individualities. *Your* Lord is he that shall deliver you out of all your troubles. Your Lord has no other business but to manifest himself to you and through you, and so make you mighty with his own mightiness made visible, whole with his health; perfect by showing forth the Christ perfection.

Let all your expectation be from your Lord. Let your communion be with him. Wait upon this inner-abiding Christ often, just as you would wait upon any visible teacher. When you are sick "wait thou only upon God" as the Most High, rather than upon healers. When you lack wisdom in small or large matters, "wait thou upon God," and see what marvelous wisdom for action will be given you. When desiring to speak the word which shall deliver another from the bondage of sickness or sin or sorrow, "wait thou upon God," and just exactly the right word will be given you, and power will go with it; for it will be *alive* with the Spirit.

SPIRITUAL GIFTS

TENTH LESSON

It is very natural for the human heart to first set out in search of truth because of the "loaves and fishes."

Perhaps it is not too much to say that the majority of people first turn to God because of some weakness, some failure, some almost unbearable want in their lives. After having tried every other way in vain to overcome or satisfy the want, they turn in sheer desperation to God.

There is, down in the hidden depths of even the most depraved human heart, though he would not for worlds have others know it, an instinctive feeling that somewhere there is a power that is able to give him just what he wants; and that if he could only reach that which to his conception is God, he could prevail upon him to grant his desires. This feeling is itself God-given. It is the Divine Self, though only a spark at the center of the man's being, suggesting to him the true remedy for all his ills.

Especially have people been led to seek the truth for the reward, or "for the work's sake," during the last few years, since they have come to know that God is not only able, but willing, to be made unto them perfect deliverance from all the burdens of their everyday life. Every one wants to be free, *free*, free as the birds of the air—free from sickness, free from suffering, free from bondage, free from poverty, free from all forms of evil; and they have a *right* to be; it is a God-given desire, and a God-given right.

Thus far nearly all teaching has limited the manifestation of Infinite Love to one form—that of healing. Sickness, incurable disease and suffering reigned on every side, and every sufferer wanted to be free. We had not yet known that there was willingness as there was power—aye, more, that there was *intense desire* on the part of our Father to give us something more than sweet, patient submission to suffering.

When the truth that Divine Presence ever lives in man as perfect life, and can be drawn upon by our recognition and faith to come forth into full and abounding health, was first taught, it attracted widespread attention, and justly so. Both teachers and students centered their gaze upon this one branch or outcome of a spiritual life, losing sight of any larger, fuller or more complete manifestation of the indwelling Father. Teachers told all their pupils most emphatically that this knowledge of the truth would enable them to heal, and they devoted all their teaching to explanation of the principles and to giving formulæ and other instructions for healing the body. And the time is now ripe for giving larger and broader views of the truth about spiritual gifts.

Healing of the body is beautiful and good. Power to heal is a divine gift, and as such you are fully justified in seeking it. But God wants to give you infinitely more.

Why should you or I limit the Limitless One to the bestowal of a particular gift, unless, indeed, we be so fairly consumed with an inborn desire for it that we are sure it is God's highest desire for us? In that case we will not have to "try" to heal. Healing will flow from us wherever we are. Even in a mixed crowd of people, without any effort of our own, the one who *needs* healing will receive it from us; that one will "touch" us, as did the one woman in all the multitude jostling and crowding against Jesus. Only one *touched* him.

Healing is truly "a branch of the vine," but it is not the only branch. There are many branches, all of which are necessary to the Perfect Vine, which is seeking through you and me to bear much fruit.

What God wants is that we shall grow into such conscious oneness with himself, such realization that he who is the substance of all good really abides *in us*, that "*ye shall ask what ye will, and it shall be done unto you.*"

If you are faithfully and earnestly *living* what truth you know, and still find your power to heal is not as great as it was at first, recognize it as all good. Be assured, no matter what any one else says to you or thinks, that the *seeming failure does not mean loss of power*. It means that you are to let go of the lesser in order that you may grasp the whole, in which the lesser is included. Do not fear for a moment to let go just this one little branch of divine power, and choose rather to have the highest thoughts of Infinite Mind, let them be what they may, fulfilled through you. We need to take our eyes off the ends of the branches, the results, and keep them centered in the Vine.

You are a vessel for some purpose. And if you let go cheerfully when the time comes, without humiliation or shame or sense of failure, your tense, rigid mortal grasp on some particular *form* of manifestation, like healing, and "covet earnestly the *best* gifts," whatever they may be in your individual case, you will do "works" in that one specific direction which will be simply marvelous in the eyes of all men. These works will be done without effort on your part, because they will be God, Omnipotent, Omniscient, manifesting himself through you in his own chosen direction.

St. Paul says: "Now concerning spiritual gifts, brethren, I would not have you ignorant. . . . There are diversities of gifts, but the same Spirit. . . . For to one is given by the Spirit the word of wisdom; to another the word of knowledge by the same Spirit; . . . to another faith; . . . to another the gifts of healing; . . . to another the working of miracles; to another prophecy; to another discerning of spirits; to another divers kinds of tongues," etc.

The same Spirit, always and forever the same, and one God, one Spirit, but in different forms or manifestation. Gift of healing no more, no greater, than the gift of prophecy; gift of prophecy no greater than faith, for faith (when it is really God's faith manifest through us), even as a grain of mustard seed, shall be able to remove mountains; the working of miracles no greater than the power to discern spirits (or the thoughts and intents of other men's hearts which are open always to Spirit). And "greatest of all these is love;" for "love never faileth" to melt down before it all forms of sin, sorrow, sickness and trouble. Love *never* faileth.

"But all these worketh that one and the selfsame Spirit, dividing to every man severally as he will. . . . For the body is not one member, but many. . . . If the whole body were an eye [or gift of healing], where were the hearing? If the whole were hearing, where were the smelling? . . . And the eye cannot say unto the hand, I have no need of thee: nor again the head to the feet, I have no need of you. . . . But now hath God set the members every one of them in the body, *as it hath pleased him.*"

Thus St. Paul has enumerated some of the free "gifts" of the Spirit to those who will not limit the manifestations of the Holy One, but yield themselves to Spirit's desire within them. Why should we so fear to abandon ourselves to the workings of Infinite Love and Wisdom! Why be so afraid to let him have his own way with us, and through us!

Has not the gift of healing, the only gift we have thus far sought, been a good and blessed one, not only to ourselves, but to all with whom we have come in contact?

Then why should we fear to wait upon God with a perfect willingness that the Holy Spirit manifest itself through us as it will, knowing that whatever the manifestation, it will be *good*—all good to us and to those around us!

Oh, for more souls who have the courage to abandon themselves utterly to Infinite Will—souls who dare let go of every human being for guidance, and, seeking the Christ within their own souls, let its manifestation be what He will!

Such courage might possibly mean, and probably would at first, a seeming failure, a going down from some apparent success which had been in the past. But the going down would only mean a mighty coming up, a most glorious resurrection of God into visibility through you in his own chosen way, right here and now. The failure, for the time, would only mean a grand, glorious success a little further on.

Do not fear failure, but call failure good; for it really is. Did not Jesus stand an utter failure, to all appearances, when he stood dumb before Pilate, all his cherished principles come to naught, unable (yes, I say it—*unable*, or else not tempted in all points as we are) to deliver himself, or to "demonstrate" over the agonizing circumstances of his position?

But had he not failed right at that point, there

never could have been the infinitely grander demonstration of the resurrection a little further on. "Except a seed fall into the ground and *die*, it cannot bring forth fruit." If you have clung to just one form of spiritual gift because you were taught that, and you begin to fail, believe me, it is only the death, the disappearance of one gift, in order that out of it may spring many new gifts—brighter, higher, fuller ones, because the ones God has chosen for you.

Your greatest work will be done in your own God-appointed channel. If you will let Divine Spirit possess you wholly, if you will *will* to have the Highest Will done in you and through you continually, you will be quickly moved by it out of your present narrow limitations, which a half-success always indicates, into a manifestation as much fuller and more perfect and beautiful as is the new grain than the old seed which had to fall into the ground and die.

Old ways must die. Failure is only the death of the old that there may be the hundredfold following. If there comes to you a time when you do not demonstrate over sickness, etc., as you did at first, do not run outside of yourself to seek some healer. It is beautiful and good for another to "heal" you bodily by calling forth Universal Life through you; but right here there is something higher and better for you.

Spirit, the Holy Spirit, which is *God in movement*, wants to teach you something, to open a bigger, brighter way to you. And this apparent failure is his call to you to arrest your attention and turn you to him. "Acquaint now thyself with him, and be at peace: *thereby* good shall come unto thee." Turn to the Divine Presence within yourself. Seek him. Be still before him. Wait upon God quietly, earnestly, but oh, *so still* and trustingly, for days—aye, weeks, if need be! Let him work in you, and sooner or later you will spring up into a resurrected life of newness and power that you never before dreamed of.

When these transition periods come, in which God would lead us up higher, should we get frightened or discouraged, and run off to seek the help of some healer to simply be made physically well, we only miss the lesson he would teach, and so postpone the day of receiving our own fullest, highest gift. In our ignorance and fear we are thus hanging on to the old grain of wheat which we can see, not daring to let it go into the ground (of failure) and *die* (or fail), lest there be no resurrection, no newness of life, nothing bigger and grander come out of it.

Oh, do not let us longer fear our God, who is All-Good, and who longs only to make us each one a giant instead of a pigmy!

What we all need to do above everything else is to cultivate the acquaintance or consciousness of the Spirit within our own being. We must *take our attention off from results, and seek to live the life.* Results will be "added unto us" in greater measure when we turn our thoughts less to the "works" and more to embodying the indwelling Christ into our entire being. We have come to a time when there must be less talking *about* the truth, less treating and being treated merely for the purpose of being delivered from some evil *result* of wrong living; there must be more *living* the truth, and *teaching* others to do so. There must be more incorporating of the truth into our very flesh and bone.

How are you to do this?

"I am the way, the truth, and the life," saith the Christ at the center of *your* being.

"I am the vine, ye are the branches: He that abideth [consciously] in me, and I in him [in his consciousness], the same bringeth forth much fruit: for without me [or severed from me in your consciousness] ye can do nothing. . . . If ye abide in me, and my words abide in you, ye shall ask *what ye will*, and it shall be done unto you."

I do assure you, as do all teachers, that you can bring *good things* of whatever kind you desire into your life by holding to them as yours in the invisible until they become manifest. But, beloved, do you not see that our highest, our first—aye, our *continual* —thought should be to seek the *abiding in him?* to seek the knowing as a living reality, not simply as a fine-spun theory that he abides in us? then ye shall ask what ye will, be it power to heal, to cast out demons, or even the "greater works" and "it shall be done unto you."

There is one Spirit—"One God and Father of all, who is above all, and through all, and in you all. But unto every one of us is given grace [or free gift] according to the measure of the gift of Christ" in us.

"Wherefore I put thee in remembrance that *thou stir up the gift of God, which is in thee.*"

Do not be afraid, "for God hath not given us the spirit of fear; but of power, and of love, and of a sound mind."

It is all one and the same Spirit. To be the greatest success, you do not want my gift, nor I yours; each wants his own, such as will fit his size and shape, his capacity and desires, such as not the mortal mind of us, but the Highest in us, shall choose. Seek to be *filled* with the Spirit; to have the soul of things incarnated in larger degree in your consciousness; it will reveal to your understanding your own specific gift, or the manner of God's desired manifestation through you.

Let us not desert our own work, our own God within, to gaze after or pattern like our neighbor, neither to seek to make his gift ours; nor yet let us criticize his failure to manifest any specific gift. Whenever he "fails," give thanks unto God that he is leading him up into a higher place, where there can be a fuller and more complete manifestation of the Divine Presence through him.

And "I . . . beseech you that ye walk worthy of the vocation wherewith ye are called,

"With all lowliness and meekness, with long-suffering, forbearing one another in love;

"*Endeavoring to keep the unity of the Spirit in the bond of peace.*"

UNITY OF THE SPIRIT

ELEVENTH LESSON

Did we not know it as a living reality that behind all the multitude and variety of human endeavors to bring about the millennium there stands forever the Great Master-Mind which sees the end from the beginning, the Great Master-Artist who himself is (through human vessels as his hands) putting here a touch of one color and there a touch of another, according to the vessel used, on the picture, we might sometimes be discouraged.

Were it not at times so utterly ridiculous, it would always be pitiful to see the human mind of man trying to limit God to personal comprehension. However much any one of us may know of God, there will always be unexplored fields in the realms of expression, and it is an evidence of our narrow vision to say, "This is all there is of God."

Suppose a dozen people are standing on the dark side of a wall in which are various sized openings. Viewing the scene outside through the opening assigned to him, one sees all there is within a certain radius. He says, "I see the whole world; in it are

136

trees and fields." Another, through a larger opening, has a more extended view; he says, "I see trees
and fields and houses; I see the whole world." The
next one, with a still larger opening, exclaims, "Oh,
you are all wrong! I alone see the whole world; I
see trees and fields and houses and rivers and ani-
mals."

The fact is, each one looking at the same world
sees just according to the size of the aperture through
which he is looking, and he limits the world to just
his own circumscribed view of it. You would say
at once that such limitation was only a mark of each
man's ignorance and narrowness. Every one would
pity the man who thus displayed—aye, fairly
vaunted—his ignorance.

From time immemorial there has been schisms
and divisions among religious sects and denomina-
tions. And now with the newer light we have, even
the light of the knowledge of one God immanent in
all men, many still cling to the external differences,
so postponing, instead of hastening, the day of the
millennium; at least they postpone it for themselves.

I want, if possible, to help break down all seeming "middle walls of partition," even as Christ, the
living Christ, doth in reality break down or destroy
all real walls of partition. I want to help you to see

that there is no real wall of difference between all the various sects of the new theology, except such as appear to you because of your circumscribed view. I want you to see, if you do not already, that every time you try to *limit* God's manifestation of himself in any person or through any person, in order to make that manifestation conform to what *you* see as truth, you are only crying loudly, "Ho, every one, come and view my narrowness and ignorance!"

I want to stimulate you to lose sight of all differences, all side issues and lesser things, and seek but for one thing—*i. e.*, the consciousness of the presence of an indwelling God in your own soul and life. And believe me, just as there is less separation between the spokes of a wheel the nearer they get to the hub, so you will find that the nearer you both come to the Perfect Center, which is the Father, the less difference will there be between you and your brother.

The Faith Healer, he who professes to believe only in what he terms "divine healing" (as though there could be any other healing than divine), differs from the so-called Spiritual Scientist only in believing that he must ask, seek, knock, importune, befor he can receive; while he of the Science teaching knows that he has *already* received God's free gift of life and health and all things, and that by speaking the words of it the gifts are made manifest. Both get like results (God made visible) *through faith in the Invisible.* The mind of the one is lifted to a place of faith by asking or praying; the mind of the other is lifted to the place of faith by speaking the words of truth.

Is there any real difference?

The Mental Scientist usually scorns to be classed with either of the other two sects. He loudly declares that "all is mind," and that all the God he knows or cares anything about is the invincible, unconquerable "I" within him, which nothing can daunt or overcome.

He talks about conscious mind and unconscious mind and subconscious mind, and fancies he has something entirely different and infinitely higher than either of the other sects. He boldly proclaims, "I have the truth; the others are in error, too orthodox," etc., and thus he calls the world's attention to the small size of the aperture through which he is looking at the stupendous whole.

Beloved, as surely as you and I live, it is all one and the same truth. There may be a distinction, but it is without a difference.

The happy Methodist who will *from his heart*

exclaim, "Praise the Lord!" no matter what happens to him, and who thereby finds "all things working together for good" to himself, is in reality saying the "All is good" of the metaphysician. Each one is simply "acknowledging Me [or God, Good] in all thy ways," which is indeed a magical wand, · bringing sure deliverance out of any trouble to all who faithfully use it.

The teachings of Spirit are intrinsically the same, because Spirit is one. I heard an uneducated little colored woman speak in a most orthodox prayer meeting some time ago. She knew no more of "science" than a babe knows of Latin. Her whole face, however, was radiant with the light of the Christ manifest through her. She told how, five or six years before, she was earnestly seeking to know more of God (seeking in prayer, as she knew nothing about seeking spiritual light from people), and one day, in all earnestness, she asked that some special word of his will might be given directly to her as a sort of private message. These words flashed into her mind: "If thine eye be single, thy whole body shall be full of light. . . . No man can serve two masters."

She had read these words many times, but that day they were illumined by the Spirit, and she saw that to have an eye "single" meant *seeing but one*

power in her life; while she saw two powers (God
and devil, Good and evil) she was serving two masters. From that day to this, though she had passed
through all sorts of troublous circumstances, and
trials of poverty, illness in family, intemperate husband, etc., she found always the most marvelous,
full and complete deliverance out of them all by resolutely adhering to the "single eye"—seeing God
only. She would not even *look* for a moment at the
seeming evil to combat it or rid herself of it, because,
as she said, "Lookin' at God with one eye and this
evil with the other is being *double-eyed,* and God
tole me to keep my eye single."

This woman, who had never heard of any "science," or metaphysical teaching, or laws of mind,
was compassing and actually overcoming all the trib-
ulations of this world by positively refusing to have
anything but a single eye. She had been taught in
a single day by Infinite Spirit the whole secret of
how to banish evil, and have only good and joy in
her. Isn't it all very simple?

At center, all is one and the same God forever
more. And I believe that the Hottentot, the veriest
heathen that ever lived, he who worships the golden
calf as his highest conception of God, worships God.
His mind has not yet expanded to a place where he

can grasp any idea of God apart from a visible form, something that he can see with human eyes and handle with fleshly hands.   But at heart *he is seeking something higher than his present conscious self* to be his deliverance out of evil.

Are you and I, with all our boasted knowledge, doing anything more or different?

The Spirit at the center of even the heathen, who is God's child, is thus seeking, though blindly, its Father-God. Shall any one dare to say that it will not find that which it seeks—its Father? Shall we not rather say it *will* find, because of that immutable law that "he that seeketh findeth"?

You have now come to know that at the center of your being God (omnipotent Power) ever lives. From the nature of your relationship to him, and by his own immutable laws, you may become conscious of his presence and eternally abide in him and he in you.

The moment any soul really comes to recognize that which is an absolute fact—*viz*., that one Spirit, even the Father, who being made manifest in the Son, ever lives at the center of *all* human beings— he will know that he can cease forever from any undue anxiety about bringing others into the same external fold as himself. If your friend, your son, your husband or brother, does not see the truth as you see it, do not try by repeated external argument to convert him.

"And I, if I be lifted up from the earth, will draw all men unto me." That which is needed is not that you (the mortal which is so fond of talk and argument) try to lift up your brother. The Holy Spirit, or Christ within him, declares, "If I be lifted up, I will *draw* him." You can silently lift up this "I" within the man's own being, and it will draw the man up unto—what? Your teaching? No. "Unto me," the divine in himself.

If your beloved one seems to you to be going all wrong, you just say nothing at all. Keep your own light lifted up by living the victorious life of the Spirit. And then, remembering that your dear one, as well as yourself, is an incarnation of the Father, keep him silently committed to the care of his own Divine Spirit. You do not know at all what God wants to do in him; you never can know.

You do know, if you have fully recognized the fact of the same God dwelling in all men as dwells in you, that each one's own Lord, the Christ within himself, will make no mistake. The greatest help you can give to any soul is to silently tell him whenever you think of him, "The Holy Spirit lives within you; he cares for you, is working in you that which he would have you do, and is manifesting himself through you." *Then let him alone.* Be at perfect rest about him, and the result will be infinitely more and better than you could have asked or thought.

Keep ever in mind that each living soul in all God's universe is a *radiating center* of the same Perfect One, some radiating more and some less, according to the awakened consciousness of the individual. If you have become conscious of this radiation in yourself, keep your thought *centered* right there, and the Spirit of the living God will radiate itself out from you in all directions with mighty power, doing without noise or words a great work in lifting others up. If you want to help others who are not yet awakened to this knowledge, center your thought upon this same idea for them—*i. e.*, that they are radiating centers of the All-Perfect. Keep your "*eye single*" for them, as did the little colored woman for herself, and Spirit will teach them more in a day than you could in months or years.

Throughout all the ages man has been prone to the idea of separateness instead of oneness. He has believed himself separate from God and separate from other men. And even in these latter days when we talk so much about oneness, most metaphysical teachers manage again to separate God's children from himself, by saying that while one suffers the other knows no suffering, nor does he take cognizance of the child's suffering.   We, his children, forever a part of himself, are torn and lacerated, while he, knowing nothing of this, goes sailing on as serenely and coldly as the full moon sails through the heavens on a winter night.

Little wonder, is it, that many to whom the first practical lessons in the gospel of the Christ came as liberation and power, should in time of failure and heartache have turned back to the old limited idea of the Fatherhood of God?

There is no real reason why we, having come to recognize God as Infinite Substance, should be by this recognition deprived of the familiar Fatherly companionship which in all ages has been so dear to the human heart.   There is no necessity for us to separate God as substance and God as tender Father; no reason why we should not, and every reason why we *should*, have both in one; they are one—God-Principle *outside* of us as unchangeable law, God *within* us as tender, loving Father-Savior, who sympathizes with our every sorrow.

There is no reason why, because in our earlier years some of us were forced into the narrow Puritanical limits, which stood for a religious belief, we should now so exaggerate our freedom as to fancy we are entirely self-sufficient, and shall never again need the sweet, uplifting communion between Father and child. The created, who ever "lives, moves, and has his being" in his Creator, needs the conscious presence of that Creator, and cannot be entirely happy in knowing God only as cold, unsympathetic principle. Why cannot both conceptions find lodgment in our minds and hearts? Both are true, and both are necessary parts of a whole. The two were made to go together, and *in the highest cannot be separated*.

God as underlying substance of all things, God as principle, *is* unchanging, and does remain forever uncognizant of and unmoved by the changing things of time and sense. It *is* true that God as principle does not feel pain, is not moved by the cries of the children of men for help. It is a grand, stupendous thought that this power is all unchanging law, just as unchanging in its control of our affairs as in the government of the starry heavens. One is fairly conscious of his entire being expanding into grandeur as he dwells upon the thought.

But this is not all, any more than the emotional side is all. True, there is law; but there is gospel also. Nor does gospel make law of none effect; *it fulfills law.* God is principle, but God is individual also. Principle becomes individualized the moment it comes to dwell in external manifestation in a human body.

Principle does not change because of pity or sympathy, "even as a father pitieth his children." The "Father in me" *always moves* into helpfulness when called upon and trusted. It is as though Infinite Wisdom and Power, who is Creator, Upholder, Father, outside, becomes transformed into Infinite Love, which is Mother, with all of warmth and tender helpfulness which that word implies, when he becomes focalized, so to speak, within a human body.

I do not at all understand it, but in some way this Indwelling One does *move* to lift the consciousness of his children up, and place it parallel with God, Principle, Law, so that no longer two are crossed, but the two—aye, the three—the human consciousness, the indwelling individual Father, and the Holy Spirit—are made *one.* In every life, with our present limited understanding (Jesus with his greater understanding was not yet exempt), there comes times when the bravest heart goes down for the moment under the apparent burdens of life;

times when the strongest intellect bends like a "reed
shaken in the wind," when the most self-sufficient
mind feels a helplessness which wrings from it a cry
for help from the "Rock that is higher than I."

Every pure metaphysician either has reached, or
must in future reach this place: the place where God
as cold principle alone will not suffice any more than
in the past God as personality alone could wholly
satisfy. There will come moments when the human
heart is so suddenly struck as to paralyze it, and for
the moment make it impossible, with strained effort,
to "think right thoughts."

At such times there will come but little comfort
from the thought, "This suffering comes as the result
of my wrong thinking; but God, my Father, takes
no cognizance of it; I must work it out unaided and
alone."   Just here we must have, and we *do* have,
the *Motherhood of God*, which is not cold principle
any more than your love for your child is cold principle.   I would not make God-principle less, but
God-individual more.

Your Lord's (the Father in you) whole business
is to care for *you*, to love you with an everlasting
love, to note your slightest cry and rescue you.

Then you ask, "Why doesn't he do it?"

Because you do not recognize his *indwelling* and

his power, and by resolutely affirming that *he does now manifest himself as your all sufficiency,* call him forth into visibility.

God (Father-Mother) *is* a present help in time of trouble; but there must be a recognition of this fact, a turning away from human efforts, and an acknowledgment of *God only* (a single eye) before he becomes manifest.

BONDAGE OR LIBERTY, WHICH?
TWELFTH LESSON

Finally, my brethren, be strong in the Lord, and in the power of his might.—Eph. 6:10.

Finally, brethren, whatsoever things are true, whatsoever things are honest, whatsoever things are just, whatsoever things are pure, whatsoever things are lovely, whatsoever things are of good report; if there be any virtue, and if there be any praise, think on these things.—Phil. 4:8.

Every soul is by nature, or believes itself to be, in bondage to the flesh and the things of the flesh. All suffering is the result of this bondage. The history of the children of Israel coming up out of their long bondage in Egypt is descriptive of the human soul, or consciousness, growing up out of the animal or sense part of man and into the spiritual part.

"And the Lord said [speaking to Moses], I have surely seen the affliction of my people which are in Egypt, and have heard their cry by reason of their taskmasters; for I know their sorrows;

"And I am come down to deliver them up out of that land unto a good land and a large, unto a land flowing with milk and honey."

These words express exactly the attitude of the

Creator toward his highest creation (man) ever since.

Today, and all the days, he has been saying to us, his children: "Surely I have seen the affliction of my people which are in Egypt [darkness of ignorance], and have heard their cry by reason of their taskmasters [sickness, sorrow and poverty]; And I am [not I will, but I *am now*] come down to deliver you out of all this suffering, and to bring you up unto a good land and a large, unto a land flowing with good things."

Sometime, somewhere, every human soul must come to itself. Having tired of eating husks it will "arise and go to my Father." "For it is written, As I live, saith the Lord, to me every knee shall bow, and every tongue shall confess to God."

This does not mean that God is a stern autocrat, who, by reason of supreme power, will compel man to bow to him. It is rather an expression of the order of divine law, the law of all love, all good. Man, who is at first living in the selfish animal part of himself, *shall* grow up through various stages and by various processes unto the divine or spiritual understanding where he knows he is one with the Father, and where he is free from all suffering, because he has conscious dominion over all things.

Somewhere on this journey the human consciousness
or intellect comes to a place where it gladly bows to
and confesses that its spiritual self, its Christ, is highest, and is Lord. Here and forever after, not with
sense of bondage, but with joyful freedom, the soul
cries out, "The Lord reigneth." Every one must
sooner or later come to this point of experience.

You and I, dear reader, have already "come to
ourselves." Having become conscious of an op-
pressive bondage, we have arisen and set out on the
journey from Egypt to the land of liberty, and now
we cannot turn back if we would. Though possibly
there will come times to each of us before we reach
the land of milk and honey (the time of full deliverance out of all our sorrows and troubles), when
we will come into a deep wilderness or up against an
impassable "Red Sea," when our principle seems to
fail, yet does God say unto each one of us, as unto
the trembling children of Israel, "Fear ye not, stand
still, and see the salvation of the Lord, which he will
show to you."

Each soul must sooner or later learn to stand
alone with its God; nothing else avails. Nothing
else will ever make you master of your own destiny.
There is in your own indwelling Lord all the life
and health, all the strength and peace and joy, all

the wisdom and support you can ever need or desire. No other can give to you as can this indwelling Father. He is the spring of all joy and comfort and power.

Hitherto we have believed we were helped and comforted by others, that we received joy from outside circumstances and surroundings; but it is not so. All joy and strength and good spring up from a fountain within one's own being; and if we only knew this truth we would know that, because *God in us* is the fountain out of which springs all our good, nothing that any one does or says, or fails to do or say, can take away our joy and good.

Some one has said, "Our liberty comes from an understanding of the mind and thoughts of God toward us." Does God regard man as his servant, or as his child? Most of us have believed ourselves not only the slave of circumstances, but also, at the best, the *servants* of the Most High. Neither belief is true. It is time for us to awake to right thoughts, to know that we are not servants, but children, and if children, then heirs. Heirs of what? Why, heirs to all wisdom, so that we need not through any lack of wisdom make mistakes; heirs of all love, so that we need know no fear or envy or jealousy; heirs of all strength, all life, all power, all good.

The human intelligence is so accustomed to the
sound of words heard from childhood, that often to
it they convey no real meaning. Do you stop to
think, to really comprehend, what it means to be "an
heir of God and joint heir with Christ"? It means,
as Emerson says, that "Every man is the inlet, and
may become the outlet, of *all* there is in God." It
means that all that God is and has is in reality for
us, his only heirs, if we only know how to *claim our
inheritance.*

This claiming our rightful inheritance, the inheritance which God *wants us to have* in our daily
life, is just what we are learning how to do in these
simple talks.

Truly Paul said, "That the heir, as long as he
is a child, differeth nothing from a servant, though he
be lord of all;

"But is under tutors and governors until the time
appointed of the father.

"Even so we, when we were children [in knowl-
edge], were in bondage under the elements of the
world:

"But when the fullness of the time was come,
God sent forth his Son. . . . And *because ye are
sons,* God hath sent forth the Spirit of his Son into

your hearts [or into your conscious minds], crying,
Abba, Father.

"Wherefore thou art no more a servant, but a
son; and if a son, then an heir of God through
Christ."

It is through Christ, this indwelling Christ, that
we are to receive all that God has and is, as much
or little as we can or dare to claim.

No matter with what object you believed you
first started out to seek the knowledge of the truth, it
was in reality because it was God's "fullness of
time" for you to arise and begin to claim your inheritance. You were no longer to be satisfied with or
under bondage to the elements of the world. Think
of it! God's "fullness of time" *now* for you to be
free, to have dominion over all things-material, to be
no longer bond servant, but a son in *possession of
your inheritance!* "Ye have not chosen me, but I
have chosen you, and ordained you, that ye should
go and bring forth fruit."

We have come to a place now where our search
for the truth must no longer be for the rewards; it
must no longer be seeking a creed to follow, but it
must be the *living a life.* In these simple lessons
we have just taken the first steps out of the Egyp-
tian bondage of selfishness, lust and sorrow, toward

the land of liberty where perfect love and all good reign.

Every right thought we think, every unselfish word or action, is bound by immutable laws to be fraught with good results. But in our walk we must learn to lose sight of *results*, which are the "loaves and fishes." We must seek rather to consciously *be* the truth, be love, be wisdom, be life (as we really are *unconsciously*), and let results take care of themselves.

Every soul *must* take time daily for quiet and meditation. In this lies the secret of power. No one can grow in either spiritual knowledge or power without it. Practice the presence of God just as you would practice music. No one would ever dream of becoming a power in music except by spending some time daily alone with music. Daily meditation alone with God seems some way to *focus* Divine Presence within us and to our consciousness.

You may be so busy with the *doing*, the outgoing of love to help others (which is unselfish and God-like as far as it goes), that you find no time to go apart. But the command, or rather the invitation, is, "Come ye apart and rest awhile." And believe me, it is the only way you will ever gain definite knowledge, newness of experience, steadiness of purpose, or power to meet the unknown which must come in all daily life. Doing is secondary to being. When we *are* consciously the truth, it will radiate from us and accomplish the works without our ever running to and fro. If you have no time for this quiet meditation, make time, take time. Watch carefully, and you will find that there are some things, even in the active unselfish doing, which can better be left undone than that you neglect regular concentrated meditation.

You will find some hours spent every day in idle conversation with people who "just run in for a few moments" to be entertained. If you can help such people, well; if not, gather yourself together and not waste a moment just idly diffusing and dissipating yourself to gratify their idleness. You have no idea what you lose by it.

When you withdraw from the world for meditation, let it not be to think of yourself or your failures, but invariably to get all your thoughts centered on God, and upon your relations to the Creator and Upholder of the universe. Let all the little sandpapering cares and anxieties go for a while, and by effort, if need be, turn your thoughts away from them to some of the simple words of the Nazarene or Psalmist. Think of some truth, be it ever so simple.

No person, unless he has practiced it, can have any idea of how it quiets one from all physical nervousness, all fear, all over-sensitiveness, all the little raspings of everyday life—just this hour of calm, quiet waiting *alone* with God. Never let it be an hour of bondage, but always one of restfulness.

Some, having realized the calm and power which come of daily meditation, have made the mistake of withdrawing themselves entirely from the world that they may give the entire time to meditation. This is asceticism, which is neither wise nor profitable.

The Nazarene, who was our noblest type of the perfect life, went daily apart from the world only that he might come again into it with renewed spiritual power. So we go apart into the stillness of Divine Presence that we may come forth into the world of everyday life with a new inspiration, and increased courage and power for activity and for overcoming.

"We talk to God—that is prayer; God talks to us—that is inspiration," says Lyman Abbott. We go apart to get still, that new life, new inspiration, new power of thought, new supplies from the Fountainhead, may flow in; and then we come forth to shed it all abroad upon those around us, that they too may be lifted up. Inharmony cannot remain in any home where even one member of the family daily practices this hour of the presence of God, so surely does the renewed infilling of the soul by peace and harmony result in the continual outgoing of peace and harmony into the entire surroundings.

Again, in this new way which we have undertaken, this living the life of the Spirit instead of the old self, we need to seek always to have more and more of the Christ spirit of meekness and love incorporated into our daily life. Meekness does not mean servility nor imbecility, but it means a spirit which could stand before a Pilate of false accusation, "opening not his mouth." No one so grand, so Godlike as he who, because he knows the truth of Being, can stand meekly and imperturbed before the false accusations of mortal mind. "Thy *gentleness* hath made me *great.*"

We must forgive as we would be forgiven. To forgive does not simply mean to arrive at a place of indifference to those who do personal injury to ourselves; it means far more than this. To forgive is to *give for*—to give some actual, definite good in return for evil given. One may say, "I have no one to forgive; I have not a personal enemy in the world." Even so; and yet if, under any circumstances, any kind of a "served-him-right" spirit springs up

within you over anything any of God's children may
do or suffer, you have not yet learned how to forgive.

The very pain you suffer, the very failure to
demonstrate over some matter which touches your
own life deeply, may rest upon just this spirit of un-
forgiveness which you harbor toward the world in
general. Put it away with resolution.

Do not be under bondage to false beliefs about
your circumstances or environment. No matter how
evil any circumstances may seem, nor how much it
may seem that some other personality is at the foundation of our sorrow or trouble, God, good and
good alone, is *real* there when you call his law into
expression.

If we have the courage to persist in seeing only
God in it all, "even the wrath of man" shall be invariably turned to our advantage. Joseph, in speaking of the action of his brethren in selling him into
slavery, said, "As for you, ye thought evil against
me; but God meant it unto good." "*All* things
work together for *good* to them that love God," or
to them who recognize only God. All things!
And the very circumstances in your life that seem
torturing, heart-breaking evils will turn to joy before
your eyes, if you will steadfastly refuse to see anything but God in them.

It is perfectly natural for the human soul to seek to escape from its troubles by running away from present environments, or planning some change on the material plane. Such methods of escape are absolutely vain and foolish. "Vain is the help of man" or mortal.

There is no permanent or real *outward* way of escape from miseries or circumstances; all must come from *within*.

The words, "God is my defense and deliverance," held to in the silence until they become part of your very being, will deliver you out of the hands and the arguments of the keenest lawyer in the world.

The real inner consciousness as a truth that "The Lord is my shepherd, I shall not want," will supply *all* my wants more surely and far more liberally than any human hand can.

The ultimate aim of every soul should be to come into the consciousness of an indwelling God. And then in all external matters affirm *deliverance* through and by this Divine One. There should not be a running to and fro of the mortal, making human efforts to aid the Divine, but a calm, restful, unwavering *trust* in All-Wisdom and All-Power within to accomplish the thing desired.

Victory must be won in the silence of your own

soul first, and then you need take no part in the outer demonstration or relief from conditions. The very walls of Jericho which keep you from your desire must fall before you.

The Psalmist said: "I will lift up mine eyes unto the hills [or to the Highest One], from whence cometh *my help*.

"My help cometh from the Lord, which made heaven and earth.

"The Lord [thy indwelling Lord] shall preserve thee from all evil.

"The Lord shall preserve thy going out and thy coming in from this time forth, and even for evermore."

Oh, if we could only realize that this mighty power to save and to perfect, to deliver and to make alive, lives forever *within* us, and so cease now and always to look away to others!

There is but one way to obtain this full realization—the way of the Christ. "I am the way, the truth, and the life," spoke the Christ through the lips of the Nazarene.

Holding to the words, "Christ is the way," when you are perplexed and confused, and can see no way of escape, will invariably open a way of complete deliverance.

When you have studied "Lessons in Truth" carefully, the Unity School of Christianity recommends to you "Christian Healing," by Charles Fillmore, an excellent course of lessons in Practical Christianity.

PUBLISHER'S ANNOUNCEMENT

Upon the title page of this volume there is printed the name of the publisher, Unity School of Christianity. Those interested in the philosophy which "Lessons in Truth" teaches will no doubt desire to know more of the School that is promulgating the doctrine of Practical Christianity. For the benefit of these, a brief history of the Unity work is here given:

The Unity School had its inception thirty years ago in Kansas City, Mo. It has always been an independent movement, not connecting itself with any other religious organization. It is a revival of primitive Christianity and teaches the science underlying the doctrine of Jesus Christ. It does not represent a new sect; its readers and followers embrace hundreds of thousands, many of whom are active in their denominational churches.

At the Unity Headquarters in Kansas City, can be found a large band of workers who are united for the one purpose of spreading the gospel of Truth, which is life and health to all people. The work of the School has developed until at the present time it occupies several large buildings.

The School publishes a monthly magazine, *Unity*, a weekly paper, a child's magazine, and numerous books, booklets and pamphlets. A complete catalogue of these publications will be sent gratis, upon request.

INDEX